W9-BYC-864

NATIONAL GEOGRAPHIC KiDS

COOK-BOOK

A Year-Round FUN Food Adventure

Barton Seaver

NATIONAL GEOGRAPHIC
WASHINGTON, D.C.

contents

Kitchen Skill Quick Reference

Hi, I'm Barton Seaver, a National Geographic explorer and chef.

When I was growing up, my parents took mealtime very seriously. In my family there was nothing more important than the moments we spent around the table, sharing food and talking about our day. But my favorite part was helping cook the meals. I was fascinated by everything—the sights and smells, as well as the variety of tastes and textures, that came through the kitchen.

Today my fascination with cooking continues to grow. I consider myself a "food explorer"—a job I've been preparing for since those early days. Ingredients on our plates today come from every corner of the globe, and just as a photograph can transport us to a faraway place, so does the food on our table. I love to dive in and embrace flavors I've never tried before and to put them together in new ways. And through these food journeys, I've discovered that simple, delicious recipes using ingredients that are fresh and in season can transform an ordinary dinner into an amazing experience.

Mealtime should involve more than just nourishing your body. It should also be about broadening your horizons and creating memories for you and your family. Just like the explorers out in the world diving the deep oceans or traversing the frozen landscape of the North Pole, you can make amazing discoveries by having an open mind and not shying away from the unknown.

As a profession, cooking has taken me all over the world. It has connected me to people and given me lasting memories that I will cherish forever. And so, I present this book in the hopes that you will embrace the ideas and challenges between these pages and start off on the food adventure of your life.

Cooking Tools

Make sure that you have all the tools you need before you start a recipe. Here's a list of each tool mentioned in the book with a picture for quick reference.

Baking Dish

Baking Tray

Blender

Butter Knife

Colander

Cooking Rack

Cutting Board and Knives

Food Processor

Grater

Hand Mixer

Ladle

Measuring Spoons

Measuring Cup (liquid)

Measuring Cups (dry)

Mixing Bowls

Meat Thermometer

Nonstick Pan

Parchment Paper

Peeler

Pot

Cooking Tools, continued

Sauté Pan

Saucepan

Spatula

Stand Mixer

Strainer

Tongs

Whisk

Wooden and Slotted Spoons

Kitchen Safety

To make cooking fun and safe for everyone, you do need to follow some important kitchen rules.

Never cook without an adult present. Things can go wrong in the kitchen and get out of hand quickly. You must have an adult nearby in case of an emergency, especially if you are working with knives or an open flame (which you must only do with a parent's permission).

Make sure you are dressed properly. Chefs wear those aprons and funny hats for a reason! Tie back your hair, roll up your sleeves, and put on an apron if you are worried about protecting your clothing.

Always wash your hands with soap and warm water before you begin cooking, and immediately after you touch raw meat, fish, or eggs.

Use oven mitts when handling hot foods and never reach over an open flame.

Always turn the handles of pots and pans in toward the back of the stove so that someone doesn't accidentally bump into them.

Use kitchen tools for their intended purpose.

Be very careful when using knives and always use a cutting board. See page 21 for specific instructions on handling knives.

Clean up as you go along.

When in doubt, ask for help! Chances are you are going to find some instructions in this book that will be unfamiliar. You should never try to guess what to do, as cooking can be dangerous. Ask an adult to help you with anything that is unclear.

Cooking Techniques

Throughout this book you'll find quick lessons on cooking basics like chopping and measuring, but here are descriptions of important techniques to know to help you along the way.

Bake: to cook food in an oven

Blanch: to boil or steam for a short time

Boil: to heat a liquid to 212 degrees

Broil: to cook food under direct heat, usually by placing it in the broiler of your oven

Brown: to turn a food lightly brown by cooking or heating

Caramelize: to slowly cook a fruit or vegetable until it becomes brown and sweet

Crush: to break an ingredient into a powder or very small pieces, often done by pressing the ingredient with the back of a spoon or the flat of a knife

Dice: to chop an ingredient into small cubes

Dilute: to lessen the flavor or thickness of something by adding another mixture or liquid

Drain: to remove the liquid while retaining the food; often done with a strainer or a colander

Drizzle: to lightly pour a small amount of liquid or oil over something

Garnish: to add an edible decoration or savory touch to a dish

Grate: to reduce an ingredient to small particles, usually by using a specially designed tool called a grater

Grill: to cook food over a fire by placing it on a metal grate

Incorporate: to gently but thoroughly combine

Juice: to remove the juice from a fruit or a vegetable; can be done by hand or with the aid of a kitchen tool

Mince: to chop into very small pieces

Peel: to remove the outer layer from a fruit, a vegetable, or other item

Preheat: to allow the oven or pan to warm up to a set temperature

Pureé: to pulverize an ingredient until it becomes a thick liquid

Sear: to quickly cook the surface of a food with intense heat

Season: to use herbs, spices, or salt to flavor foods

Shave: to remove a thin layer (or layers) of an ingredient

Shred: to tear or cut into long, thin pieces

Simmer: to heat a liquid so that it is almost boiling for an extended period of time

Steep: to soak a flavoring ingredient in liquid for an extended period of time

Toss: to combine the ingredients together in a bowl so that they are evenly mixed

Whisk: to mix with a quick, sweeping stroke

New Year's Party

Snow Day Snacks

Play With Your Food!

January always arrives with a great sense of excitement. The rush of the holidays is over, and we can finally reflect upon our goals for the upcoming year. We often use this time to commit ourselves with renewed enthusiasm to things we want to accomplish, and we are full of optimism about what the coming year will bring. The possibilities are endless! Because it's the start of a brand new year, January 1 is full of traditions from all over the world that are said to bring good luck and health. **In this chapter you'll read about a few of my favorites!**

new year's **party**

Sparkling Cider

The highlight of every New Year's party is toasting the arrival of midnight. Start things off right by making this fun and fancy drink. It's super easy and sure to impress! Any sparkling juice will do, but I like apple cider best. The flavors really come alive when spruced up with the jazzy aromas of citrus and cinnamon.

Prep: 5 minutes / Serves: 1

5 ounces sparkling apple cider

1 strip lemon zest (peel)

1 strip orange zest (peel)

1 cinnamon stick

1 Slowly pour the cider into a fun glass so that it doesn't foam up.

2 Using a vegetable peeler, remove a strip of the peel from a lemon and another strip from an orange. You want to have one long strip, about 2 inches long, so go slowly and don't press too hard or you will get too much of the bitter white skin, known as the pith. Take the citrus peels and wrap them around the cinnamon stick.

3 Place the cinnamon stick on the rim of the glass and serve immediately. Before you take a sip, dunk the cinnamon stick into the glass and give it a quick stir to combine the flavors. Enjoy!

RINGING IN THE NEW YEAR is a tradition all on its own. The holiday can be traced all the way back to more than 3,000 years ago! Today, everyone celebrates differently. Some people light fireworks, some dine on special foods or beverages, some people give gifts, and many cultures toast the New Year on completely different dates. But no matter when or where, New Year's is always a celebration! How do you toast the New Year?

Black Bean Soup

Bean dishes have been associated with New Year's celebrations for thousands of years. In Japan, the traditional dish of choice is a black soy bean soup called *kuromame.* Typically eaten over the first three days of a new year, the beans are thought to promote hard work and good health. This recipe calls for canned black beans, but you can cook with dry beans if you want, either by soaking them in cold water overnight, or by covering the beans with water and bringing them to a boil on the stove, then letting them sit for an hour.

Prep: 10 minutes (longer if using dried beans) / Cook: 20 minutes / Serves: 4

2 tablespoons cooking oil (canola or vegetable)

1 onion, peeled and diced

1 green pepper, seeds removed and diced

1 large carrot, peeled and diced

1 teaspoon ground cumin

1 bay leaf

3 cups vegetable broth or water

2 cans (15 ounces each) low-sodium black beans, drained and rinsed

salt

1 In a large pot, heat the oil over medium heat and add the diced vegetables. Cook for 5 minutes, stirring every minute or so, or until the onions and peppers are beginning to soften.

2 Add the cumin and bay leaf and stir until mixed well. Add the broth or water and the beans.

3 Reduce the heat to low and simmer for 10 minutes or until the carrots are soft. Remove the bay leaf and discard. Season with salt and serve.

TRY THIS!
THIS SOUP IS GREAT WITH A DOLLOP OF SOUR CREAM ON TOP.

Hoppin' John

Need a little extra cash this year? Try eating Hoppin' John, a traditional New Year's dish that arrived in the American South along with the colonists in the 1700s. Hoppin' John is thought to bring wealth and prosperity—the round black-eyed peas represent coins, and the greens of the stew symbolize the green color of American money!

Prep: 10 minutes /
Cook: 35 minutes / Serves: 4

4 strips bacon, cut into thin slivers

1 small onion, peeled and diced

1 green pepper, seeds removed and diced

2 stalks celery, cut into thin slices

2 cans (15 ounces each) black-eyed peas, drained and rinsed (or 2 pounds frozen black-eyed peas)

1 cup water

salt

1 In a large pot over medium heat, cook the bacon slivers until they are just beginning to crisp, about 5–7 minutes. You will not need to stir them very often.

2 Add the diced onion, pepper, and celery slices and continue to cook over medium heat for another 10 minutes or until the celery begins to soften.

3 Add the beans and the water, season with salt, and stir to combine. Reduce the heat to low and cover the pot. Cook for 20 minutes and then remove it from the heat. The mixture should be slightly thickened. Serve hot!

CUISINE SCENE

The Southern United States

Food tradition is alive and well in the southern United States—an area rich with local culture. The history of this region is a mixed bag of people from many other countries and continents who significantly influenced the dishes that come from this area. Many of the ingredients used in southern cooking were introduced by settlers who brought them from native countries. From African ingredients brought over with the slave trade to French-influenced cuisine brought by the Cajuns as they migrated south from French Canada, the flavors are bold yet comforting. Southern cuisine, traditionally rich and wonderfully flavored with onions, tomatoes, peppers, and okra (to name a few), mirrors the charming, gracious, and welcoming culture of this dynamic mix of people.

BLACK-EYED PEAS GET THEIR NAME FROM THE BLACK SPOT THAT RESEMBLES AN EYE.

EATING BLACK-EYED PEAS IS THOUGHT TO BRING GOOD LUCK IN MANY CULTURES AROUND THE WORLD.

new year's party

CHOCOLATE HAS BEEN INCLUDED IN EVERY AMERICAN AND RUSSIAN SPACE VOYAGE.

Milk Chocolate Panna Cotta

New Year's food might be rooted in tradition, but you can top off your feast with a fancy dessert just for fun. Panna cotta is a traditional Italian dessert (*panna cotta* means "cooked cream"). It is similar to pudding but has a thicker, richer texture and taste, making it a great way to end your celebration. It is so easy to prepare—the hardest part is having the patience to let it chill!

Prep: 15 minutes / Chill: 4–5 hours /
Serves: 4

¼ cup milk

1 envelope unflavored gelatin

2 cups heavy cream

2 tablespoons sugar

1 teaspoon vanilla extract

1 cup milk chocolate chips

YOU MIGHT LOVE CHOCOLATE NOW, BUT CHANCES ARE YOU WOULDN'T HAVE TOUCHED IT HUNDREDS OF YEARS AGO! UNTIL RECENT HISTORY, CHOCOLATE CONTAINED NO SUGAR AND WAS SERVED AS A BEVERAGE!

1 Pour the milk into a small bowl, and stir in the gelatin until it's fully combined. Allow the mixture to sit for 5 minutes for the gelatin to soften (or "bloom," as it is often called). In a small saucepan, heat the cream, sugar, and vanilla until hot (but not boiling). Remove the pan from the heat and add the chocolate chips. Whisk gently until all the chocolate has melted into the cream and there are no lumps. Make sure to scrape the base of the pan, where bits of unmelted chips can hide!

2 Using a spatula, add the gelatin mixture to the chocolate sauce and stir to combine. Pour the mixture into 4 coffee cups or small bowls. Carefully place the dishes in the fridge and allow to cool for at least 4–5 hours so that the gelatin has time to cool and thicken the dessert.

3 Serve in the cup or bowl and garnish with fresh fruit and whipped cream, or just enjoy the panna cotta on its own.

Healthy Eating

Healthy eating is not a complicated idea. A healthful diet is one that includes a diversity of foods and is rich in vegetables, whole grains, fruit, and healthy proteins. But it is not all or nothing. Healthy eating takes into account all the choices we make for our meals. Not every meal or ingredient has to be perfectly healthy for us. It is a balance between the choices we make. When your mom says, "No dessert until you finish your green beans," it's because she knows that it's okay to treat yourself a little bit, as long as you're getting the nutrients your body needs, and not overdoing it. Most important of all is that we enjoy the food we eat and that it makes us feel good and energized.

snow day snacks

You know the feeling—you wake up on a cold, dreary January morning, absolutely dreading the thought of walking out into the freezing temperature to wait at the bus stop. You drag yourself out of bed, pull back the curtains ... and ... SNOW! Pure, white, magical, sweet, school-canceling snow blankets the world outside. You run through the house rejoicing and envisioning the endless possibilities that await you. But then 2 p.m. hits. You've built a snowman, sledded down a hill 20 times, constructed a fort, won your snowball fight, and now you're just bored—not to mention hungry! So what's next? Snow day snacks—delicious munchies that take very little prep and can be eaten with one hand while you throw a snowball with the other!

Dinosaur Kale Chips

These crunchy snacks are super simple to make. All it takes is a few minutes to pull the stems from the kale and you're ready to roll! It is important that you use a specific kind of kale known as dinosaur kale. It has this great name because the leaves look like dinosaur skin! This variety is also known as black, Tuscan, or lacinato kale, depending on where you live.

Prep: 10 minutes / Cook: 40–50 minutes / Serves: 4

2 bunches dinosaur kale

1–2 tablespoons olive oil (enough to coat the kale)

salt

1 Preheat your oven to 350 degrees. Thoroughly wash and dry the kale. Next, strip the stems from the kale by holding the stem and running your fingers gently up the stalk in order to separate the leaves. Throw the stems away or save them for the next time you make veggie soup.

2 Toss the kale leaves with the oil in a bowl, mixing thoroughly to ensure that each leaf is evenly covered.

3 Season the leaves with a little salt and place them on a large baking tray. Place the tray in the oven and cook for 25 minutes.

4 Take the tray from the oven and toss the leaves using tongs to expose the parts that are still droopy. Place the tray back in the oven and cook for another 15–25 minutes, or until the kale is evenly crispy throughout. These are best when eaten right out of the oven.

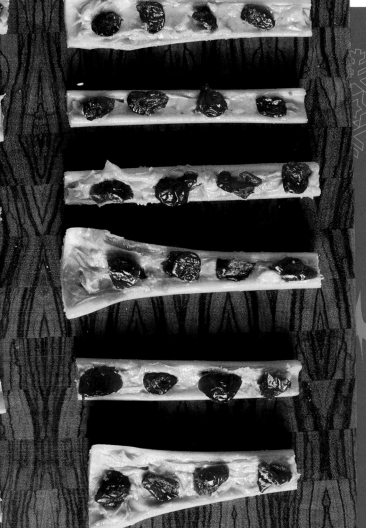

Ants (and Fire Ants) on a Log

This classic snack with a creepy name is an easy way to prepare a healthy and delicious afternoon treat. There are many variations of this, so try using your favorite ingredients along with those in the recipe below to create a mixed platter. (And don't worry, no real ants are harmed in the making of this dish.)

Prep: 20 minutes / Serves: 4

6 stalks celery, washed and cut into 3-inch sections

½ cup peanut butter or almond butter (I prefer chunky)

2 tablespoons raisins (for ants)

2 tablespoons dried cranberries (for fire ants)

1. Using a butter knife, spread the nut butter into the celery sticks.

2. Garnish each stick with a few of the raisins and cranberries. You can alternate the raisins with cranberries on each log or you can keep them separate.

Washing Fruits and Veggies

Washing produce is an important step in the preparation of any meal. Before you begin to cook, thoroughly wash the fruits and vegetables that you will be using under cold running water. Use your fingers to gently brush the surfaces of the produce to remove any grit or residue from chemicals used in the growing process. After you've washed them, either shake them dry to remove the water or pat them dry with paper towels. With delicate fruit, such as strawberries, gently place the fruit in a colander and wash with cold water. Allow the fruit to drain until dry before using.

TRY THIS! WANT TO SWITCH YOUR ANTS UP? USE BANANA CHIPS, CHOCOLATE CHIPS, OR DRIED APRICOTS CUT INTO SLIVERS.

REAL ANTS ARE SOMETIMES USED IN SALADS AND CURRIES, OR EATEN ROASTED BY THEMSELVES!

challenge

Play
With Your Food!

Snow day snacks are the perfect way to crack up while you fuel up! Now that you know how to make some of my favorite snow day snacks—like Dinosaur Kale Chips and Ants on a Log—your challenge is to come up with your own creative concoction. See if you can make edible caterpillars (hint: start with a banana), cauliflower sheep, or marshmallow snowmen. Even better, grab a friend or family member, and create his or her likeness out of fruit and veggies!

Marshmallow Snowmen

When it's too cold to make real snowmen outside, try making some edible versions in front of a toasty fire. These guys are the ultimate way to have fun with your food—and they're easy to make! Marshmallows will harden when left out, so they make cute wintery decorations ... or you can just eat them right away, of course.

Prep: About 5 minutes, or as long as you want!

Marshmallows (try using different sizes, like jumbo, regular, and mini)

Toothpicks

Frosting

Candy for decorating—I use M&Ms and Red Hots, but your imagination is the limit!

1 Assemble your snowmen using the marshmallows and toothpicks. You can use different sizes for the body, head, and arms, or do whatever you like!

2 Now decorate your snowmen! You can use pretzels for arms, licorice for candy scarves, candy for hats, or whatever else you can dream up. Frosting helps secure the candy to the marshmallows.

3 You're finished! You can display your snowmen as awesome snowy decorations, play with them, or eat them. If you do decide to snack on your creations, just make sure to remove the toothpicks first.

KITCHEN SKILL

How to Use a Knife Knife skills are absolutely essential for any cook. The first skill to learn when using a knife is how to not cut yourself! Always be conscious of the knife and how you hold it. Never point with a knife, and when walking with a knife, make sure that the tip is always pointing down. A sharp knife is absolutely essential. Here's why: A knife is a tool meant to do the work for you. A sharp knife slides right through food, making a clean and easy cut. Dull knives won't cut so easily and therefore require the chef to use pressure to attempt to force the knife through the ingredient. When you exert pressure, you can lose control, and the knife can slip and cut you. Get a sharp knife and let the knife do the work for you!

Another important thing to remember is that you are trying to cut the food—not yourself—so keep your fingers protected. The best way to do this is to grip the item to be cut with your fingers curled inward so that the knife can lean against your knuckle. This not only helps guide the knife to cut where you want it to, but it also keeps your fingertips safely away from the blade.

Valentine's Day Dinner

Make a 3-D Valentine!

Soup Off!

February, I find, is a month that begs us to stay indoors. The short, cold days give way to bitterly frigid nights, and we find comfort in the warmth of the kitchen. The foods we crave are rich and filling. It is a great month to snuggle up in the company of family and celebrate being together. February also brings Valentine's Day and a chance to use food to show our affection for those we love. What better way to show someone you care than by preparing a delicious meal? In this chapter, you'll read a few of my favorite recipes to cook for others. **Try them out and see what your family thinks!**

valentine's day dinner

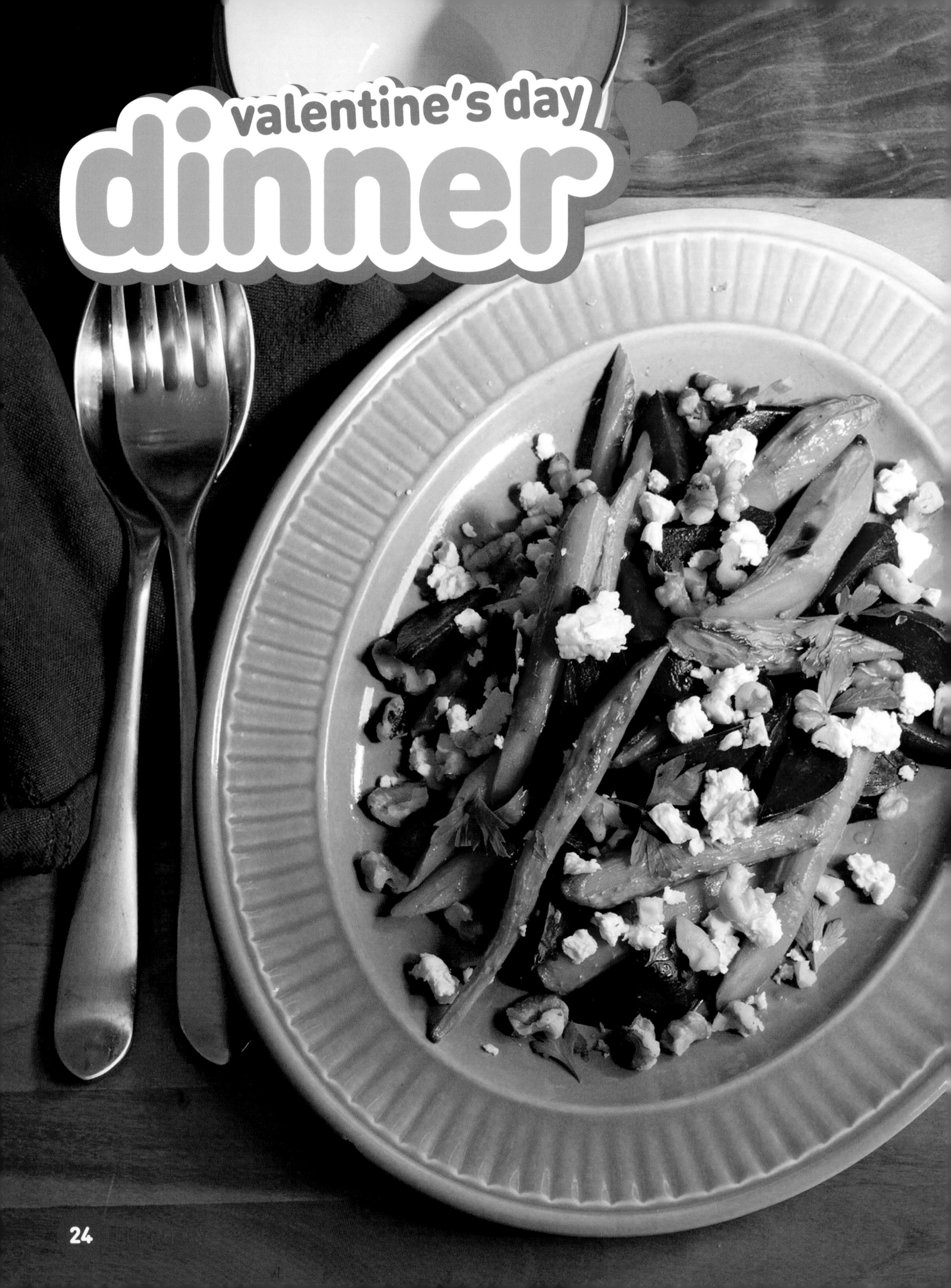

Celebration Salad

When planning your Valentine's Day menu, choose fruits and vegetables with vivid colors to add cheer to a generally dreary month. If you are squeamish about unknown veggies, give them a try just once. The beets you may have tried in the past were most likely from a can. Fresh beets have a mild flavor and a delicious crunch. With the salty bite of feta cheese and crunchy walnuts, this salad is a feast for the eyes and the mouth!

Prep: 20 minutes /
Cook: 40 minutes / Serves: 4

1 pound beets, washed

salt

½ pound carrots, peeled and cut into 3-inch segments

2 tablespoons olive oil

¼ cup walnut pieces

¼ cup crumbled feta cheese

1 lemon, cut in half

a few parsley leaves (optional)

1 Place the beets in a pot and cover them with water. Season the water with a generous amount of salt and then place the pot over medium heat. Simmer for about 20–25 minutes, depending on the size of the beets, until you can easily pierce one with the tip of a knife. Drain and allow the beets to cool slightly.

2 Place the carrots in a pot and cover them with cold water. Season with salt and place over high heat. When the water comes to a boil, reduce the heat to low and cook for another 5 minutes, or until the carrots are tender when pierced with a knife. Drain and let cool.

3 Peel the beets using a few layers of paper towel to rub off the skins. This can get a little messy, so be sure to wear an apron and use extra paper towels if necessary. If there is a little peel left on the beets, it is not a problem. Throw the skins away.

4 Preheat the oven broiler to high. Cut the beets into small slivers and place them in a large ovenproof sauté pan (one with no plastic parts). Add the carrots to the pan and then add the olive oil and toss to coat evenly. Place the whole pan under the broiler and cook until the vegetables begin to brown and sizzle, about 5–10 minutes.

5 Remove from the oven with some help from an adult. Transfer the vegetables to a large platter. Garnish the salad with a sprinkling of salt, walnuts, and the crumbled feta cheese. Drizzle with lemon juice and scatter parsley leaves over the top. Serve warm.

The Science of Sweet

Humans evolved as hunter-gatherers, which basically means that we had to either hunt or find our food. It was a lot of work! Our early ancestors spent so much energy just trying to find their food that they developed a taste for easy-to-eat, sweet, ripe fruits. The stored energy in sugar is much easier for our bodies to process and requires less energy to access. That's why it's called a sugar rush—a burst of energy. Even as we evolved past finding our food, we still maintained our sweet tooth—a preference for the sugar-filled foods that make us feel happy. For a dessert that will satisfy your cravings, check out page 30.

valentine's day dinner

KITCHEN SKILL

Seasoning With Salt

Many recipes will tell you to season "to taste." This is because "taste" is different for everyone. When you are seasoning food, it is important to learn how to find that balance of tasty but not too salty. Try this trick to learn how much salt is to your taste. Put a few potatoes (peeled and cut into chunks) in a saucepan and cover them with water. Bring them to a boil, then reduce the heat and let them simmer for about 20 minutes, or until you can easily pierce them with a fork. Drain the potatoes and allow them to cool, then mash with a fork. Separate out about half the potatoes and begin to season that half with salt, measuring as you go. Keep adding small amounts, tasting as you go, until you get the potatoes just right. Then add a little more salt until they taste too salty. By doing this, you will learn how much is too much, and you will be better able to season "to taste" from now on. But be sure not to waste your potatoes: Simply add them back into the other half and mix to combine so that you dilute the salt. Season again using the skills you just learned, add butter and milk if desired, and enjoy!

PEOPLE IN THE U.S. SEND ABOUT A BILLION VALENTINE'S DAY CARDS EACH YEAR.

THERE ARE TWO TOWNS IN THE U.S. NAMED VALENTINE—ONE IN NEBRASKA AND ONE IN TEXAS.

Joaquin
I ♥ U

Roasted Lemony Chicken Breasts

Valentine's Day calls for a dish that looks so sophisticated that no one will know it took only a few minutes to put together. The rosemary and the sour lemon in this chicken recipe are the perfect match.

Prep: 5 minutes / Cook: 25 minutes / Serves: 4

2 large or 4 small chicken breasts, boneless and skinless

salt

1 tablespoon olive oil

2 stalks fresh rosemary

1 lemon sliced into thin rounds

1 Preheat the oven to 400 degrees. Season the chicken with salt. In an ovenproof sauté pan (one with no plastic parts) heat the oil over medium heat.

2 Add the rosemary and cook for 1 minute. Add the chicken breasts directly on top of the rosemary and cover them with the lemon slices.

3 Place the whole pan in the oven and cook for about 20 minutes, until the chicken has reached 160 degrees on a meat thermometer. If you don't have a meat thermometer, then go ahead and cut one of the breasts open to reveal the inside. It should be white all the way through with no signs of pink.

4 Remove the pan from the oven and let it sit in a warm place for 5 to 10 minutes. This allows the chicken to continue to cook as well as to absorb some of the delicious cooking juices. Serve the chicken with the lemon slices and the crispy rosemary as garnishes.

valentine's day dinner

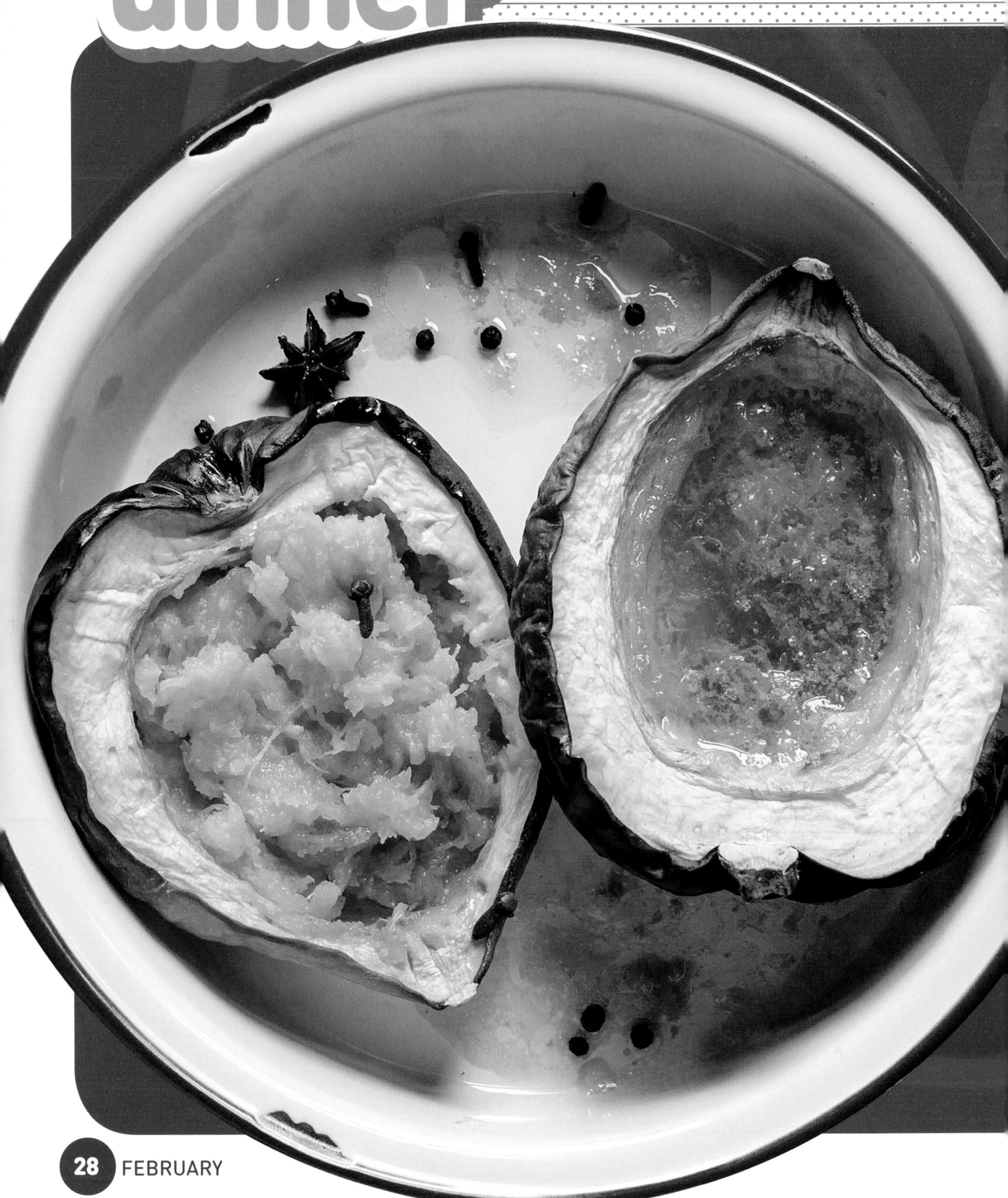

Roasted Acorn Squash Hearts
with honey butter and spices

Like pumpkin pie? Then you'll love this tasty dish! Roasting sweet acorn squash is so easy, and the results are delicious. The squash provides its own cooking vessel as it roasts right in the skin—and when cut in half, it looks like a heart! It's the perfect Valentine's Day treat!

Prep: 5 minutes / Cook: 40–50 minutes / Serves: 4

2 acorn squash (about the size of a softball)

4 tablespoons butter

4 tablespoons honey (or maple syrup)

1 pod star anise (or 2 teaspoons powdered cinnamon)

4 cloves (or 2 teaspoons) grated nutmeg

salt

1 Preheat the oven to 350 degrees. Have your parents cut the squash in half from top to bottom. Scoop out the seeds and discard. Pierce the squash with a fork a few times to let the steam release. Place the halves cut side up in a baking dish.

2 Put 1 tablespoon of butter and 1 tablespoon of honey (or maple syrup) into the cavity of each half. Put a piece of the star anise pod (or ½ teaspoon of cinnamon) and a clove (or ½ teaspoon of nutmeg) in each half. Season with salt and place the dish into the oven.

3 After about 40–50 minutes, the squash should be tender and you should be able to shred the flesh using a fork. Remove it from the oven. Remove the star anise and cloves from the cavities and use a fork to scrape the meat from the squash, though keeping it in the shell. Carefully mix to incorporate the butter and honey (or maple syrup). Serve hot.

EDIBLE
WEATHER
REPORT

When Belgium introduced the endive to Paris, it became so popular that it was called "white gold."

The first recorded mention of okra comes from a Spanish traveler who visited Africa in 1216.

Carrots are not indigenous to America; they arrived with the pilgrims.

Dal is the Hindi word for lentils and also refers to a traditional spiced lentil stew.

◉ Root Crops
IDAHO & MAINE, U.S.A.

Endive
BELGIUM

Lentils
◉ **INDIA**

Okra
ETHIOPIA ◉

Raspberry Yogurt Parfait

Top off your fancy meal with a satisfying dessert that you can make in advance. For this dish, you sweeten thick and creamy Greek yogurt with maple syrup or honey and add fresh or frozen fruit for a sweet and sour punch. The crunchy granola topping adds a fun crunch to each bite.

Prep: 15 minutes / Serves: 4

2 cups plain Greek-style yogurt

3 tablespoons maple syrup or honey

¼ teaspoon vanilla extract

1 cup raspberries, fresh or frozen

½ cup granola

1 In a bowl mix the yogurt with the maple syrup or honey and the vanilla and stir well to incorporate.

2 Spoon the yogurt mixture into 4 serving glasses, filling each up about halfway. Place a ring of raspberries on top of the yogurt in each glass.

3 Fill up the glasses with the remaining yogurt. Top each glass with the remaining raspberries and then add the granola in the center of each glass. Serve chilled.

green scene

Make a 3-D Valentine!

Be sweet to your loved ones and the Earth this Valentine's Day by turning everyday items around your house into something heartfelt. Show how much you care about the environment by creating recycled cards for your family and friends.

YOU WILL NEED

- old newspaper or leftover tissue paper
- heart-shape cookie cutter
- a clean plate
- bowl of water
- paintbrush
- glue wash (equal parts glue and water)
- an old greeting card

WHAT TO DO

1 Tear newspaper or tissue paper into small pieces. Place the cookie cutter on the plate. Making sure each piece overlaps, position a few pieces of the paper inside the cookie cutter to create a thin layer. Dip your finger into the bowl of water and then press it gently on the paper layer, making the paper damp. Continue layering, dipping, and pressing until the cookie cutter is about half full. Let it dry for at least a day.

2 When the paper mold is completely dry, gently press down on the mold and carefully lift off the cookie cutter. Using a clean paintbrush, apply a light coat of glue wash to the mold. As it dries, move on to Step 3.

3 Cover an old greeting card with things from around the house—such as construction paper, magazines, newspapers, or doilies. Write a poem or message inside the card and then glue the 3-D heart to the front. Now you're ready to give this Earth-friendly valentine to someone you love!

challenge

Soup Off!

Soup is one of the most satisfying foods you can eat, especially in cold weather ... and let's face it, February can get cold. *Really cold.* Can you think of a better way to warm up? But before you reach for that soup can, keep in mind that soup is one of the easiest things to make, and you have to follow only a few simple rules. See my Basic Soup recipe opposite to see how it all comes together. When you feel you've mastered the art of crafting soup, follow the instructions below to hold your own Soup Off! challenge!

1 Grab a pal. A brother or sister will work nicely.

2 Grab 2 pots and start with a broth—any flavored liquid made from vegetables or meat—in each. You probably already have vegetable, chicken, or beef broth somewhere in your cupboards or freezer.

3 Let the challenge begin. Dig through your freezer, produce drawer, and cupboards for ingredients. Keep points to see who builds a better soup. Here's the point breakdown:

Each veggie is worth 3 points.

Each legume (bean) is worth 2 points.

Each grain or pasta or protein (meat or bean) is worth 1 point.

Keep a record of your creations so that you can keep perfecting your recipe!

Basic Soup

To make a veggie soup, start by gathering the ingredients that you want to use and some store-bought veggie broth. Putting the soup together is as simple as organizing your ingredients in order of how long they take to cook. Follow these rough guidelines for putting the soup together.

1 Start by bringing the broth to a simmer over medium heat (use about 1½ cups of broth per person you plan to serve).

2 Next, add your dry ingredients and simmer until they are cooked: quinoa, noodles, rice, lentils, etc.

3 Add your hard vegetables and simmer until they are cooked: celery, onions, carrots, turnips, green beans, etc. You want to have about a 50:50 ratio of broth to veggies.

4 Last, add in the soft vegetables that only really need to warm through: mushrooms, peas, cabbage, tomatoes, zucchini, and frozen vegetables.

5 Once the soup comes back to a simmer, taste to check the seasoning and add salt if necessary. Serve immediately.

March can be a moody month. One day it is raining and cold; the next it is as sunny and warm as can be. It is a month that marks the transition between the cold winter and the hint of green spring. The foods of March follow the same pattern. We want fresh ingredients and light, playful meals. But the cool nights keep us hungry for something hearty as well. Because of the promise of warm weather, March is a time of new beginnings in cultures all over the world. Many have traditional dishes that celebrate this time of renewal, **so what better time to host an international feast?**

international feast

Mediterranean Hummus

This staple of Mediterranean cuisine has become hugely popular in America in the past couple of decades. The creamy spread, made of pureed chickpeas (a type of legume, or bean) and olive oil is a nutritious and easy-to-prepare treat. The key ingredient is a paste called tahini, made of pureed sesame seeds, which adds a wonderful depth of flavor.

Prep: 20 minutes / Serves: 4

2 cans (15 ounces each) low-sodium chickpeas (also known as garbanzo beans), drained and rinsed

1 clove garlic, peeled and minced

1 lemon, juiced

½ cup tahini paste (stirred well)

¼ cup water

salt

½ cup olive oil (or vegetable oil if you prefer a milder taste)

1 Place the chickpeas in a food processor along with the garlic, lemon juice, tahini paste, and water. Carefully turn on the machine and process until the ingredients become a thick paste. You may need to stop the machine and scrape down the sides with a spatula to make sure that the mixture is blending evenly.

2 Add a good pinch of salt to the mix and then continue to process while slowly drizzling in the oil until the paste is thick and creamy. Check the seasoning and adjust with more salt if necessary.

3 Place the hummus in a bowl and serve at room temperature with an assortment of pita chips or tortilla chips and some crunchy vegetables: celery, carrot sticks, green beans, peppers, or anything else that you can think of!

TRY THIS!
GARNISH HUMMUS WITH A TABLESPOON OF OLIVE OIL OR A SPRINKLING OF PAPRIKA.

international feast

West African Mafe

I spent a lot of time traveling in Africa, and this *mafe* (mah-fey) was one of my favorite dishes that I discovered there. It is a traditional stew in the western countries such as Senegal and can be made in many variations, but this is my favorite. Don't let the peanut butter in this dish scare you off. Peanuts and peanut butter are used in savory dishes all over the world—they add amazing flavor!

Prep: 15 minutes / Cook: 40 minutes / Serves: 4–6

1 tablespoon vegetable or canola oil

1 small onion, diced

1 green bell pepper, diced

2 cloves garlic, peeled and minced

2 tablespoons fresh ginger root, peeled and grated

1 pound ground beef (10–20% fat)

½ cup chunky peanut butter

1 pound okra (frozen or fresh), cut into small pieces

1 can (28 ounces) roasted tomatoes (best to use peeled tomatoes)

1 cup water

salt

rice, cooked according to package directions (optional)

few sprigs cilantro or parsley for garnish (optional)

1 In a large pan, heat the oil over medium heat. Add the onion and green pepper and cook until they begin to soften, about 5 minutes. Add the garlic and ginger and stir to combine well. Cook for another 3 minutes.

2 Turn the heat to high, add the ground beef, and stir to incorporate. As soon as the beef begins to brown, reduce the heat to low and add the peanut butter, okra, tomatoes, and water. Stir to combine.

3 Cover the pot and cook for approximately 30 minutes, or until the okra is soft, stirring occasionally to prevent it from burning on the bottom.

4 Season the dish with salt. Serve over rice or enjoy plain. Garnish with the cilantro or parsley, if desired.

Okra is thought to have originated in Africa and been brought to America, where it has long been a staple in the traditional southern diet. The seeds act as a natural thickener, adding great texture to soups and stews.

Peanut Allergy

Many people suffer from allergies to certain kinds of foods, and those allergies can cause very serious reactions. An allergy to peanuts has become common, and many chefs and cooks take great care to ensure that the meals we serve are safe and healthy for our guests. Here are two simple steps to avoiding a disaster at dinnertime:

1 Check with your dinner guests to make sure they don't have an allergy to peanuts or any ingredient you plan to serve at your meal.

2 If they do have an allergy to something you plan to serve, never fear! There are many ways to create delicious meals using substitute ingredients. Don't hesitate to experiment. You might even discover something more delicious!

PEOPLE PROFILE

George Washington Carver

George Washington Carver was a pioneer in American agriculture. He spent his career encouraging small farmers to plant a variety of crops that would not only provide food for their families but also improve the quality of the soil. In the late 1800s, cotton was the major money-making crop on plantations in the South. But there was a problem: When cotton was planted in the same fields year after year, it robbed the soil of important nutrients. Dr. Carver was able to show that by planting other crops like peanuts in the fields, the condition of the soil could be improved, and the crops would grow to be healthier and more plentiful. Not only was Dr. Carver's work revolutionary to the science of agriculture; he also made his discovery at a time when laws limited the rights of African-American men and women. Dr. Carver bravely broke down the racial barriers that divided our society.

Italian Asparagus Salad With Parmesan

Spring marks the rebirth of the land. The lifeless fields of winter begin to sprout up the first shoots of green. One of my favorite early-season ingredients is asparagus. These tender yet crisp stalks are incredibly versatile and go well with a lot of different foods. Here's a classic Italian pairing that I find delicious.

CHEW ON THIS

PARMESAN CHEESE is often called the "King of Cheeses." And while the name is often applied to any grated, salty cheese, true Parmesan comes from only one small region of Italy, where its traditional recipe has been passed down for hundreds of years. The cheese is made in giant wheels weighing 80 pounds or more!

The name **ASPARAGUS** comes from the Greek word meaning "sprout" or "shoot."

Prep: 5 minutes / Cook: 10 minutes / Serves: 4

1 pound asparagus

salt

1 lemon, juiced

2 tablespoons extra virgin olive oil

1 tablespoon mustard, grain or Dijon

2 ounces Parmesan cheese, either grated or shaved with a peeler

⅛ cup of red onion, peeled and sliced as thinly as possible

1 Bring a large pot of water to a boil over high heat. While the water is heating, trim the asparagus by gently bending each stalk at the base area. The stalk will break at just the right point where it becomes tender, separating from the tough, chewy base.

2 Generously season the boiling water with salt and then drop the asparagus into the water. Cook for about 2 minutes and then drain the water. Lay the asparagus on a tray to cool down, but do not refrigerate it.

3 Make a vinaigrette by combining the lemon juice, oil and mustard with a pinch of salt and mixing vigorously. Set aside until just before serving.

4 Arrange the asparagus on a platter and spoon the vinaigrette over the dish. Finish by topping each plate with a bit of the Parmesan cheese and the red onion slices. Serve at room temperature.

French Puff Pastry Napoleon

In France, puff pastry is used in everything from breakfast pastries to savory suppers, and especially desserts. It can be quite tricky to make from scratch. But guess what? You can find it premade in the freezer section of the grocery store! So why not take a quick shortcut to create a simple dessert that will look like a work of art? It requires just a few ingredients and a steady hand.

Prep: About 30 minutes /
Serves: 4

1 package frozen puff pastry, thawed

2 cups whipping cream

4 tablespoons powdered sugar

1 teaspoon vanilla extract

1 pound fresh strawberries, washed and stems removed

1 lemon, juiced

2 tablespoons cocoa powder for garnish (optional)

1 Carefully unroll a sheet of puff pastry and cut across the middle width- and lengthwise so that you have 4 pieces. Follow the instructions on the package to bake until it's golden brown. Remove from the oven and let cool. Pull the pastry apart so that you have 2 layers.

2 In a mixer (or a bowl if you are using a hand mixer), place the cream, 2 tablespoons of the powdered sugar, and the vanilla extract. Mix on high until the cream is fluffy and stiff enough that it forms "peaks." This means that the whipped cream is stiff enough that it will make a peak when you lift the mixer out.

3 Slice the strawberries into thin pieces and mix them with the remaining 2 tablespoons of powdered sugar and the lemon juice. Allow to sit for 10 minutes so the sugar begins to draw out the fruit juice.

4 Gather 4 plates. Spread a thin layer of the whipped cream mixture in the center of each plate. Top with a scoop of the strawberries and then another layer of the whipped cream. Place a piece of pastry on top of the cream. Repeat the process until you have a beautiful layered dessert with the crisp pastry as the top layer. Spoon any remaining strawberry juice around the plate and sprinkle with cocoa powder or powdered sugar if you like. Enjoy!

green

scene

Grow an Indoor Herb Garden

Make food taste even better and help the environment by planting an herb garden at home. You'll spice up meals and cut back on the pollution released into the atmosphere when trucks transport food over long distances. So go green by putting your green thumb to work.

basil

dill

Chives

Italian parsley

- empty recyclable cans
- sandpaper
- scissors
- scrap construction paper or wrapping paper
- glue
- stickers, markers, or ribbons
- small stones or marbles
- potting soil
- herb seeds
- water
- labels
- wooden craft sticks

WHAT FOODS GO BEST WITH MY HERBS?

Basil: pizza, spaghetti
Cilantro: salsa
Dill: veggie dip
Mint: iced tea
Oregano: tomato sauce
Parsley: potatoes, stuffing
Rosemary: chicken
Thyme: meatballs

WHAT TO DO

1. Remove the can labels and wash and dry the empty cans. Ask a parent to help you use sandpaper to carefully smooth any rough edges inside the open cans.

2. Cut enough scrap paper or wrapping paper to fit around the outside of the cans and glue it in place. Decorate the paper with stickers, markers, or ribbons.

3. Place a layer of small stones or marbles in the bottom of the cans for drainage. Add potting soil until the cans are ¾ full, then pat down the soil.

4. Gently press a few seeds into the dirt and cover them with soil. Lightly water the seeds, and put your herb containers in a sunny spot.

5. Attach labels to wooden craft sticks and position them in the cans.

6. Your herbs should sprout within 7 to 10 days.

KITCHEN SKILL

Blanching Vegetables Blanching is a technique that is used to prepare vegetables so that they can be finished using other cooking methods, such as grilling or sautéing. To blanch vegetables, bring a pot of water to a rolling boil and generously add salt. Put the vegetables in the water and cook for about 2 to 5 minutes, depending on their size. As soon as the vegetables begin to soften, drain them from the water and lay them on a tray to cool. You can dunk the veggies into a bowl of ice water to immediately stop the cooking, or you can place them in the fridge to cool. Either way, it stops what is known as carry-over cooking, when foods continue to cook even after they are removed from the heat and can end up mushy. This cooling stage is not always necessary but can help you get your vegetables to turn out just right.

March challenge

What's Your Green Tally?

March is often represented by the color green, so what better challenge than a green tally? Challenge yourself to try as many different green vegetables as you can!

Because of their nutritional value, green vegetables are some of the healthiest foods you can eat. Why should you care? Well, get a load of this—spinach is full of healthy vitamins and minerals and can help you have clear skin and healthy hair. Artichokes can aid digestion, can lower your cholesterol, and are great for your liver. And broccoli is rich in nutrients that can help prevent diabetes, cancer, and other harmful diseases! Plus, eating healthy is the best way to stay strong and feel great.

So, are you ready to take the What's Your Green Tally challenge? Here's what you do:

1. Go to your local grocery store and write down the names of all the green vegetables you see.

2. Go home and search for recipe ideas. (Cookbooks, magazines, and the Internet are all great resources.)

3. Plan a couple of meals around those vegetables, and ask an adult to help you cook up a few green concoctions in the kitchen.

4. Score yourself 1 point for each green veggie you eat in March.

5. On the last day of the month, count 'em up and see where you fall on the Veg-O-Meter!

Brussels Sprouts

Green Beans

Fennel

Zucchinis

Squashes

Artichoke

Green Pepper

Lettuce

Broccoli

Cucumbers

Chard

Cabbage

VEG-O-METER

0–10 Points

Pass the meat, please!

You're a true carnivore. Or possibly a "carb-o-vore," but one thing is true: You sure don't love your veggies. Did you pick at your peppers? Get grossed out by green beans? Maybe you just haven't met your match yet. Next month, try branching out to vegetables you've never tasted before. Ask a parent to pick up some of those weird-looking zucchinis. Or maybe try the kale everyone is talking about. After all, you don't know that you don't like something if you've never tried it!

10–20 Points

I'll take one of everything, please!

You are one well-rounded individual. Sure you'll tuck into a stack of pancakes, but you'll also indulge the voice of reason in your head that's telling you to go cuckoo for carrot sticks as an afternoon snack. You know that variety is the name of the game, and everything is best in moderation. So go ahead, chow down on that hamburger, champion of the clean plate club ... but just remember to eat broccoli for dessert.

20–30 Points

Peas are the only things that please!

Ugh. Mechanically separated poultry paste? I think not. Your body is a temple, and nothing is passing through your lips that doesn't grow in the ground. And while a volume of veggie is great, just make sure that you're getting the nutrients you may be missing out on by favoring one food group. Beans, nuts, and whole grains are great ways to energize your body while putting your veggie-lovin' mind at ease.

APR

Egg-stravaganza!

Breakfast Block Party

Fruit Salad Face-Off!

46

April, in many parts of the world, is the month to come out of hibernation. The first few months of the year can seem long and cold, but in April, you finally begin to feel like braving the outdoors again. The sun is shining a little bit longer, green leaves are first appearing on the trees, and the world wakes up! New life is everywhere. In April, you want to make sure you have a good breakfast to fuel you for the day ahead. At breakfast, you can explore new ingredients and old favorites. **And one of my favorite ingredients gets the spotlight this month: eggs!**

egg-stravaganza!

Eggs are a dish that just about anyone can master. But they can also be a little tricky if you don't know how to prepare them properly. Here are three classic ways of preparing eggs that will make your parents think you're the new king or queen of the kitchen:

Scrambled Eggs

This is the easiest way to cook eggs and is the best method when you're cooking for a large group, because you can make one batch to serve many. The key to good scrambled eggs is to cook them in a nonstick pan over medium heat.

Prep: 5 minutes / Cook: 5 minutes / Serves: As many as you like; use 2 eggs per person

eggs

salt

pepper

¼ tablespoon butter for every 2 eggs used

whole grain toast (optional)

1. Crack the eggs into a bowl, making sure to remove any pieces of shell that might have fallen in. Season the eggs with salt and pepper and then whisk to break up the eggs and to fully incorporate the seasonings.

2. In a nonstick pan, heat the butter over medium heat until it starts to foam but not brown. Add the eggs and stir constantly using a heat-proof spatula, gently lifting and mixing the eggs. By stirring constantly, you prevent the eggs from sticking to the bottom and overcooking. Good scrambled eggs should be fully cooked but should still have a creamy consistency. As soon as the eggs are cooked, transfer them from the pan onto a platter or individual plates. Serve with toast if you like.

Poached Eggs

Poaching is submerging whole eggs in hot water. The egg whites cook and form a softly textured ball around the yolk. You can cook poached eggs so that the yolk is either soft and runny (which makes a great sauce for your toast) or until it is solid. You will need teacups (one for each egg) and a slotted spoon for this recipe.

Prep: 5 minutes / Cook: 10 minutes / Serves: As many as you like; use 2 eggs per person

eggs

water

3 tablespoons apple cider vinegar

salt

1. Fill a large pot with water and place it over medium heat. The best temperature for poached eggs is 165–180 degrees. You can gauge this by using a meat thermometer, or judge it by sight—it's when the water is steaming but not boiling. When the water is just about right, add the vinegar and a pinch of salt. (Don't turn off the burner or the temperature will drop!)

2. Crack each egg into its own teacup (one with a handle). Carefully dip the teacup into the water to fill the cup and gently firm up the egg.

3. Once the egg white begins to turn slightly opaque, after about 20 seconds, pour the egg from the cup into the water to cook. For an egg with a runny yolk, cook for about 4 minutes, and for a fully set yolk, cook for about 7 minutes.

4. Gently remove the egg with a slotted spoon and place onto a few layers of paper towels to dry off any excess liquid. Immediately transfer to a plate for serving.

egg-stravaganza!

Sunny-Side Up Eggs

This is the prettiest way to serve eggs. The pearly egg whites frame the beautiful yellow yolks. When done properly, the yolks will be thick but still runny, providing a delicious sauce for toast. The edges of the egg whites will be slightly browned and have a hint of crisp. The keys to success are to use medium heat and to have patience. A nonstick pan is also essential!

Prep: 5 minutes / Cook: 10 minutes / Serves: As many as you like; use 2 eggs per person

½ tablespoon butter per 2 eggs

eggs

salt

pepper

1 In a small nonstick pan, heat the butter over medium heat until it starts to foam but not brown.

2 Crack the eggs directly into the pan and give the pan a very gentle shake to make sure that the eggs don't stick. Now is the time to channel your inner yoga instructor and meditate for a few minutes. Don't mess with the eggs at all! Just let them cook. The whites will turn opaque and firm up completely in about 5 minutes. The yolk will ever so slightly change color as it begins to firm up. If the edges start to brown, reduce the heat to low to even the cooking pace.

3 When the eggs are cooked to your liking (and the yolk is as runny or as firm as you like it) remove them from the pan by gently tipping it over a plate and allowing the eggs to slide off onto the dish. Season the eggs with a little salt and pepper. Serve immediately.

EGGS are usually laid by female birds and reptiles, and they have been eaten by humans for thousands of years. If you're from the United States, you're likely used to eating chicken eggs. But people around the world eat all sorts of eggs, including quail eggs, duck eggs, ostrich eggs, and even roe—fish eggs! Expand your horizons and see what kind of eggs you think are eggs-traordinary!

Anatomy of an Egg

What's inside that eggshell? Oftentimes we just crack the egg and don't think twice about it. But I challenge you to take a minute and study this wonderful food. Under the shell are two parts of the egg that we commonly refer to: the white and the yolk. The white is made up of what is called albumen, a protein. While clear when raw, it lives up to its name and cooks to a pearly white. The yolk is the yellow ball in the center. The color of the yolk depends on what the hen ate and gets its color from naturally occurring compounds. When eggs are fresh, the white is very firm and stands stiff next to the yolk.

THE TRADITION OF DECORATING EGGSHELLS CAN BE TRACED BACK AS FAR AS 60,000 YEARS AGO.

EDIBLE WEATHER REPORT

Hummingbirds are prohibited in Hawaii because they interfere with pineapple pollination.

The word "artichoke" originated in Arab-occupied Spain between the 8th and 15th centuries.

White asparagus is so popular in Germany that there is a name for its harvest season: *Spargelzeit*.

Pomegranates originated in the Middle East but grow well in South Africa, which has a similar climate.

Pineapples
HAWAII, U.S.A.

Artichokes
SPAIN

Asparagus
GERMANY

Pomegranates
SOUTH AFRICA

breakfast
block party

Breakfast is a great way to bring your friends together, and the egg dishes on pages 49–50 are super easy to make for a crowd. Why not throw a breakfast block party before everyone rushes off to soccer practice, dance lessons, hula hooping competitions ... (you get the idea)? Here are two more recipes for a fast and easy breakfast that you can cook up for the whole gang.

Deviled Eggs

This picnic favorite is a delicious way to introduce eggs as a snack anytime of the day, and is also a great idea for a portable breakfast on the go. I particularly like the challenge of peeling the boiled eggs, revealing the perfect egg hidden beneath the shell.

Prep: 15 minutes / Cook: 10 minutes / Serves: 4

6 eggs, in the shell

2 tablespoons apple cider vinegar

2 tablespoons mayonnaise

2 teaspoons yellow mustard

salt

paprika for garnish (optional)

1 Place the eggs in a small pot just large enough to hold them. Cover with water and the vinegar (which helps make the peeling process a little easier) and place the pot over high heat.

2 Once the water comes to a boil, reduce the heat to low and cook for 7 minutes. Remove the pot from the heat and carefully drain the water.

3 Allow the eggs to cool for a few minutes and then begin to peel them. It is important that the eggs are still slightly warm, as this makes the task much easier. Gently crack the shell and then carefully peel it all off in sections. Wash the peeled eggs with water to make sure that all shell fragments have been removed.

4 Cut the eggs in half lengthwise. Carefully scoop out the yolks and place them in a mixing bowl. When all the yolks have been removed, mix them with the mayonnaise, mustard, and salt. Mash with a whisk until they form a creamy paste.

5 Spoon the yolk mixture into the egg white halves, placing a small dollop right in the center of each. Garnish with the paprika (if using) and serve.

TRY THIS! LIKE YOUR EGGS WITH A LITTLE MORE PIZZAZZ? DRESS THEM UP BY ADDING OLIVES OR SWEET PICKLE TO THE MIX. A FEW DASHES OF HOT SAUCE WILL ADD A KICK OF SPICE. OR THROW IN SOME HONEY MUSTARD OR PESTO TO GIVE IT ZEST-O! JUST STIR YOUR ADD-ONS INTO THE YOLK MIXTURE AND YOU'RE GOOD TO GO!

So-Easy-
You-Can-Make-It-in-
Your-Sleep Oatmeal

Oatmeal comes in many forms—from the instant microwavable pouches to the very slow-cooking Irish style. More often than not, we don't have time to watch our breakfast simmer away for 45 minutes, so we look to convenient recipes and instant oatmeal. There is nothing wrong with that. In fact, I will take it one step further. Instead of cooking the oatmeal the morning of, try soaking the oats overnight in juice or milk. When you wake up in the morning, this delicious dish will be waiting for you to eat right away.

Prep: 5 minutes / Chill: Overnight / Serves: 4

2 cups quick oats

3 cups liquid (can be a mix of water, milk, apple cider, etc.)

fresh fruit for garnish (I love plums and strawberries for this)

maple syrup

1 The night before you want to serve this, mix the oatmeal with the liquid of your choice in a bowl. Stir well to combine. Cover and place in the refrigerator overnight—yup, it's that easy!

2 In the morning, remove from the fridge and stir. Divide into bowls and garnish with the fruit. Drizzle with a little maple syrup and serve. If you want to heat your oatmeal in the microwave, I recommend adding a few tablespoons of water.

TRY THIS! YOU CAN ADD ANY SORT OF NUT TO THIS, OR WHEAT GERM, HONEY, YOGURT, ETC. YOUR MIX-INS ARE UP TO YOU AND YOUR IMAGINATION.

Food for Your Garden!

Grow a healthy garden and reduce waste by using leftovers to make your own compost. Compost is organic material that adds nutrients to the soil. By composting, you reduce the need for chemical fertilizers in your yard and send less waste to landfills. Yard trimmings and food scraps make up about 25 percent of the trash from cities and towns in the United States. So put that banana peel to good use. Turn it—and a lot of other things in your trash can—into environmentally helpful compost. By making natural fertilizer, you will help the environment and develop your green thumb!

COMPOST THIS

For a successful compost, you need two different types of matter, called "brown" materials and "green" materials. The labels have nothing to do with the color of the items you are composting; they have to do with the items' organic composition. "Green" materials are high in nitrogen; "brown" materials are high in carbon. For a great garden, you'll need some of each. Here's a quick list to give you an idea of what falls into these two categories:

"BROWN" MATERIALS	"GREEN" MATERIALS
dead leaves	grass clippings
eggshells	fruit and vegetable scraps
twigs	coffee grounds
shredded newspaper	tea bags
nutshells	

WHAT TO DO

1 Choose a dry, shady spot to create your compost pile.

2 Use a bin with a tight-fitting lid and plenty of airholes to hold your compost ingredients. In the bin, start with a 6-inch layer of dry "brown" material (see examples in list above). Break down large pieces before you place them in the bin.

3 Add a 3-inch layer of "green" materials (see list). Add a little bit of soil to this layer.

4 Mix the brown and green layers. Finish with another 3-inch layer of brown materials.

5 Add water until the contents are moist. If you accidentally add too much water, just add more brown materials to the bin. Mix your compost pile every week or two.

6 After 1–4 months the compost will be almost ready. When it is dark brown and moist, and you can't identify the original ingredients, wait 2 more weeks. Then add your finished compost to your garden.

About That Juice You're Drinking ...

Did you know that eating whole fruits is better for your body than drinking fruit juice? When a fruit is juiced, a lot of the pulp can be lost, which is bad because the pulp slows down the absorption of sugars and nutrients to give us lasting energy and nutrition. Without it, fruit juice becomes just a big glass of sugar! Recent studies also show that eating whole fruit can lower the risk of diseases such as diabetes. Plus, nothing tastes fresher or more flavorful than a juicy piece of fruit. So put down your OJ and start a new morning tradition of eating an orange alongside a glass of water.

challenge

Fruit Salad Face-Off!

How many fruits does it take to make one awesome salad? Well, that answer is all up to you. This month's challenge is to make the most jam-packed, mouthwatering, fruitiest fruit salad you can. To get started, simply visit the grocery store produce aisle and see what looks good. Look for the basics, then branch into the unknown. Also, fresh fruits can be expensive when out of season, so you can boost your breakfast with frozen fruits. Fruits destined for the freezer aisle are picked riper than those headed for the produce aisle. Greater ripeness equals more sweetness and better flavor! So making a mix of fresh and frozen fruits can be a real winner. You can cut up the fruit and leave it as is, or add in a splash of orange or apple juice, coconut flakes, or whatever suits you that day. So where's the challenge? Well this one is for your family:

1. First you mix up a tasty fruit salad the night before and stick it in the fridge. Come family breakfast time, surprise!

2. Pop quiz. Take turns around the table and have everyone name a fruit or other ingredient in your concoction.

3. Each family member gets 1 point per correct answer. The winner gets to finish the bowl!

Edible Treats

Make a Birdbath

Farmers Market Name Game

May is when the world blooms. The birds are singing, and the warmth in the air is here to stay. The days become longer, urging us to stay outside for just a few more minutes. Seasonal farmers markets pop up in neighborhoods and on street corners, bringing fresh ingredients into our lives. And May gives us something else that's very important: a reason to celebrate our moms—or grandmas, or friends, or neighbors, or really anyone in our lives who makes us feel cared about. So while you're enjoying spring, pop in the kitchen to cook up a **treat to express thanks to those who do so much for you.**

edible treats

Zucchini Bread

The name of this treat might lead you to believe it's a savory dish, but don't let it fool you. Zucchini bread is just as moist, sweet, and delicious as its banana bread cousin—and if you've never tried it, you're missing out! I like to slice the bread, lightly toast it, and serve it with a pat of butter. This particular recipe comes from my mother-in-law, who has been perfecting it for many years. I'm very proud to pass it along to a whole new generation of admirers!

Prep: 30 minutes / Cook: 1 hour /
Makes: 1 loaf

2 eggs

1 cup sugar

½ cup cooking oil

1 cup grated zucchini (about 1 medium zucchini grated on the large hole of a box grater)

1½ cups flour

1 teaspoon baking soda

1 teaspoon salt

⅛ teaspoon baking powder

1½ teaspoons cinnamon

½ cup walnut or pecan pieces

1 teaspoon butter or oil for greasing the loaf pan

1 Preheat the oven to 350 degrees. In a large bowl, beat the eggs, sugar, and oil until fully incorporated. Add the grated zucchini and mix. Add the flour, baking soda, salt, baking powder, cinnamon, and nuts. Mix well and pour into greased 9-by-5-inch loaf pan. Bake for 1 hour. Test to see if it is done by inserting a toothpick directly into the center of the loaf. If it comes back clean, then the bread is ready. If there is a little batter on the toothpick, bake it for another 5–10 minutes and then check the doneness again.

2 Remove from the oven and let the bread cool on a rack. Carefully remove it from the pan and cut it into thick slices. Toast the slices and serve with a pat of butter on top!

THE FIRST MOTHER'S DAY was celebrated in West Virginia in 1908, when Anna Jarvis held a memorial for her mother. Mother's Day became a recognized holiday in the United States in 1914, and later spread to other countries. Though the modern version of Mother's Day is relatively recent, celebrations of mothers have occurred around the world for thousands of years.

Awesome Oatmeal Cookies

When it comes to an edible gift, nothing beats a classic cookie. They're yummy and easy to make, and they travel well—you can even pack them up in a box and ship them to a faraway friend! Moist, chewy oatmeal cookies are one of my favorites. This classic snack can be made in many ways to include your favorite ingredients, such as raisins or dried cranberries. I like to include a few walnuts in mine to give them extra crunch and added nutritional value.

Prep: 30 minutes / Cook: 15 minutes per batch / Makes: 24 cookies

1 cup raisins

1 cup butter

1 cup brown sugar

1 teaspoon vanilla extract

3 eggs

2½ cups flour

1 teaspoon salt

1 teaspoon cinnamon

2 teaspoons baking soda

2 cups old-fashioned oats

¾ cup pumpkin seeds or walnut pieces (optional)

1 Put the raisins in a small pot and cover with water. Bring to a boil and then remove from heat. Let sit for 5 minutes then drain. Set the raisins off to the side.

2 In a mixer (or bowl if you are using a hand mixer), combine the butter and sugar. Beat on medium speed until all the sugar has been incorporated (this step is called creaming the butter). Add the vanilla extract and then, with the mixer running on low speed, add the eggs one at a time, waiting till each egg is fully incorporated before adding the next one. In a separate bowl, mix the flour, salt, cinnamon, and baking soda and stir to combine. Add this dry mixture to the butter and eggs in small batches so that it incorporates fully. When all the flour mixture has been mixed in, add the raisins and the oats, and gently stir with a wooden spoon to combine.

3 Preheat your oven to 350 degrees. Let the batter sit for 10 to 15 minutes while the oven heats up.

4 Scoop small dollops of the dough onto a large cookie tray, leaving plenty of room between each. Place in the oven and bake 12 to 15 minutes. You'll know your cookies are done when they have browned slightly around the edges. Remove from the oven and use a spatula to transfer the cookies to a cooling rack. Repeat this step until all the dough is baked.

CHEW ON THIS

RAISINS
It takes four tons of grapes to make one ton of raisins.

BROWN SUGAR
Brown sugar is just white sugar mixed with molasses.

CINNAMON
Cinnamon is the inner bark of trees in the cinnamon family. In some ancient civilizations it was more valuable than gold.

OATS
Oats used to be considered a nuisance weed. They were pulled from the ground and burned.

Fruit Smoothie

Next time you want to make your mom or dad breakfast in bed, forget the pancakes—who really wants syrup on their sheets? This delicious fruit smoothie is easy to make and fits neatly into a glass that's easily carried to its destination. I prefer to use frozen fruit for these because I never know when the urge to make them will strike. I usually have a few bags of fruit in my freezer, like mango, blueberry, strawberry, and maybe even some pineapple. That's why there really is no set recipe for this, just some simple guidelines. The yogurt gives your smoothie a nutritional boost and a nice, creamy consistency. The only tool you need is a good blender that has enough power to turn the fruit into a creamy puree.

Prep: 15 minutes / Serves: 1

½ cup yogurt

½ cup fruit juice

1 cup fruit of your choice

1 I find it best to put a little liquid in the blender first, as this helps get the fruit pureed. I often add orange or apple juice, but any kind of juice will work—cherry, pomegranate, grape, you name it! I also like to include a bit of fresh fruit if I have it, especially bananas, which add a great texture to the drink.

2 The hardest part of making a smoothie is not making too much! So it helps to have someone to share your creation with. Just a little bit of fruit goes a long way. Any leftover smoothie will keep in the fridge for up to 3 days and will just need to be whipped up again before serving.

KITCHEN SKILL

How to Measure Recipes often need to be very precise, especially those for baked goods, so measuring is important. The tools for measuring are likely already in your kitchen, so grab them from the drawer and learn how to use them.

To ensure that you are measuring accurately, you must fill each measure to the brim. For liquid ingredients, fill the measure while holding it over your recipe. For dry ingredients such as flour, fill the measure over the brim and then use a table knife to scrape off the excess, giving you just the amount called for.

Make a Birdbath

When it comes to giving a gift, nothing beats a homemade present that will get the whole family outside in nature. Even better is a gift that will bring nature right to you! Have you ever noticed birds using fountains in parks as birdbaths? Well, here's one that you can make on your own. Then the whole family can go outside to watch the birds splish and splash!

YOU WILL NEED

3 terra-cotta planters of various sizes

1 flower pot saucer that is a few inches larger in circumference than the smallest flower pot

paint

paintbrush

heavy-duty outdoor glue

SOME BIRDS— LIKE QUAIL—BATHE IN THE DIRT! This prevents their feathers from getting oily. Wrens and sparrows often take a water bath and follow up with a dust bath.

WHAT TO DO

1 Experiment with different ways of making the base: Turn one terra-cotta pot upside down and then stack another right-side up on top of it. Then place the large saucer on the top pot. Or turn three different-size pots upside down and stack them in descending order, placing the saucer on top.

2 Once you decide on a shape for your birdbath, it's time to start painting! Spray paint or any other outdoor paint will work. Ask an adult for help. Choose a variety of colors. Try using a small paintbrush to add some designs to make your birdbath unique!

3 Once the paint on the pots and saucers is dry, have an adult use outdoor permanent glue to attach the pieces in the design you've chosen.

4 When the glue is dry, fill up your birdbath with water! Remember, the water in the shallow saucer will evaporate quickly. Keep it filled so the birds can swoop in to freshen up!

PEOPLE PROFILE

Sam Kass

Sam Kass is the executive director of the Let's Move! campaign and the senior policy adviser for nutrition policy at the U.S. White House. He became a chef by training at some of the finest restaurants all over the world. A Chicago native, Sam was asked by the Obama family to cook at White House functions in addition to preparing meals for the first family. Sam oversees Let's Move, which is a national effort to encourage children to exercise and eat nutritious, healthy meals that will help them thrive not only in school but also in life. Sam also oversees the White House garden and helps connect Americans to healthy food choices. In working to improve the general health of Americans, he has become a very influential voice in showing that our health is directly linked to the foods that we eat. Most important, Sam's work reminds us that sitting down to a meal can be the best part of our day.

Farmers Market
Name Game

May is a great time to reconnect with your neighbors. A wonderful way to do that is by visiting your local farmers market—and it beats trudging to the grocery store any day of the week. This time of year, no matter where you live—whether it's in a city, a suburb, or the countryside—chances are there's a place close by where you can pick up fresh-from-the-local-farm fruits and vegetables! But there are so many varieties of freshly grown food (and maybe even some fresh-baked pies or home-cured meats), and you may be wondering where to start. That's where this month's challenge comes in. In May, your goal is to try as big of a variety of different farmers market offerings as you can. Here's how:

1 On a sheet of paper (or poster board if you want it big enough to display your achievements for the whole family), list in a vertical row each letter of the alphabet. If you make a big chart, duplicate it on a regular piece of paper so your chart can travel with you.

2 Ask a trusted adult to take you to your local farmers market (it shouldn't take much persuading). Be sure to bring your chart with you.

3 See how many different fruits and vegetables you can find that start with each of the letters. When you match a letter with a food, write the name of that food in the space next to the letter (bonus points if you've never heard of that food before).

4 Try each new food. You can either purchase a piece of each food that you find (you can do this over multiple trips, so you don't have to haul all your finds home at once), or if there are free samples available, you can also check it off the list!

5 See how many letters you can get in one month. If you don't complete the whole alphabet, don't worry. Farmers markets have different selections as the seasons progress, so while you may not be able to get a "Q" in May, wait until September and grab yourself a quince!

ONE OF THE BEST PARTS OF A FARMERS MARKET is getting to know your neighbors, so you and your family can do a bonus "Name Game" by introducing yourself to the producers at the market, then see how many names you can remember.

Grilling 101

Ocean Alert!

Protein Power-Up

June means freedom. School is out for three whole months, and the days are yours. The endless summer bike rides and dips in the pool probably leave you wondering if it could possibly get any better. And when the sun starts to fade and it cools off a little, it's time to fire up the grill. Grilling can reconnect us with the simple act of cooking—that is, applying heat to food. In a kitchen, it's easy to light the stove and not think twice about it. But with the grill, we have to purposefully tend to a fire and coax it along until it's ready and **we finally get to celebrate and enjoy the food that cooks over it.**

grilling 101

How to Grill

First and foremost, you should never mess around with the grill (or fire) unless you have an adult directly present with you. Got your adult? Good. Here we go!

When most people cook over a grill, they think they need a big fire. But the best part of grilling is actually the smoke—it gives the food a bold, natural taste. Cooking over a fire is the only method in which heat itself is an ingredient that enhances the taste of the food.

Unlike using an oven (where heat surrounds your food), when you cook on the grill, you are only cooking from the bottom up. That's why you have to flip the hamburger to get it to cook evenly. But that's where it can get a bit tricky. You don't want to cook the food entirely over high heat. That will char the outside and leave the inside raw, or if it's cooked through, dry. But you also don't want it to cook low or it won't get that nice crisp on the outside. Here's how you can perfectly cook your food over a charcoal or gas grill.

1 Place all the charcoal to one side of the grill. If using a gas grill, turn one side to high and leave the other side on low. This method, called indirect grilling, creates a range of temperatures that allows you to cook with much more control.

2 Place your food over the high heat. Once it gets a little color on the outside, move it to the cooler side of the grill to cook slowly through. By cooking it gently, your food will be moist and juicy. Plus you can multitask! If the hot spot on your grill is not occupied by burgers, then you can cook vegetables such as corn and kale over the searing heat to get a delicious charred crunch.

Slow-Grilled Fish

Fish is one of the best foods that you can cook on the grill. It's healthy and versatile—meaning you can play around with lots of different flavors and marinades. This is my favorite method for cooking delicate fish, especially fillets of fish like salmon and tilapia. But this is more of a technique than a set list of ingredients, so you can add your own favorite flavors! (If you're stuck for ideas, it will pair nicely with the lemon sauce on the next page).

Prep: 5 minutes / Cook: 10–15 minutes / Serves: 4

4 fillets of fresh fish such as salmon or tilapia (about 4 ounces per person)

1 tablespoon oil (olive or vegetable)

salt and pepper

1 Ask an adult to help light the fire using the indirect method described at left. Lightly oil the fillets and season with salt and pepper (or spices of your choice).

2 Place the fillets on the grill as far from the hot spot as possible. Close the grill's lid to capture the heat.

3 The cook time is a little tricky, and depends on the size and shape of your grill and the thickness of the fish. Measure the fish beforehand and cook roughly 10 minutes per inch. But you'll want to check it occasionally.

4 When it is fully cooked, the fish should flake apart when you press on it with a fork. Serve immediately.

Grilled Lemon Sauce

This is one of my absolute favorite sauces. It can be used on fish and chicken—and even veggies! Plus it couldn't be simpler to make. Next time you are grilling a dish, why not throw a few lemons on with it?

Prep: 5 minutes / Cook: 15 minutes / Serves: 4

2 lemons, cut in half

2 tablespoons olive oil

salt and pepper

1 Place the lemon halves over the hottest part of the fire. Cook until the lemons caramelize (brown on the edges) and begin to soften, about 15 minutes.

2 Gently remove the lemons from the grill and allow them to cool for a few minutes. Squeeze the juice into a small bowl and remove any seeds.

3 Mix with the oil and a little salt and pepper—and voilà! A sauce fit for any meal.

HORACE MANN, AN EDUCATION REFORMER, INVENTED SUMMER BREAK IN 1840.

IT'S THOUGHT THAT LYNDON B. JOHNSON, THE 36TH PRESIDENT OF THE UNITED STATES, HOSTED THE FIRST BARBECUE AT THE WHITE HOUSE.

Grilled Peaches

What? Grilled fruit? Yep! You read that right. Firing up the grill is not just for dinner. There are also some delicious desserts that go great on the grate! When fruit is just coming into season and is not quite fully ripe, giving it a turn over the hot coals can cook the fruit, concentrating the delicious flavors and making it taste even sweeter. Scoop on a little ice cream, and you just found your new favorite sweet treat. Peaches are my personal favorite fruit to grill, but grilled watermelon, mangoes, apricots, pears, and even some varieties of apples can be delightful.

Prep: 5 minutes / Cook: 45 minutes / Serves: 4

4 peaches, cut in half, pits removed

1 pint ice cream (vanilla is usually the best bet, but try out a few other flavors to see what you like)

① Once you are done cooking dinner on the grill, carefully scrape down the grates with a wire brush to remove any bits of remaining food.

② If you are using a charcoal grill, place the peaches cut side down on the hottest part of the fire and then cover the grill. Ask your parents to help close all the airflow holes to slowly cook the peaches as the fire dies out.

③ If using a gas grill, place the peaches over low heat and cover the grill. The fruit should be done in about 30–45 minutes. It is best to start the cooking before you sit down to your meal so that when you are done eating, dessert is ready for you! (But be sure to keep an eye on them.)

Easy
Caesar Salad

Few salads are as popular as this classic combination of salty, crunchy, cheesy ingredients. In this recipe, I call for a store-bought dressing, as it can be a little complicated to make the dressing from scratch. But it is worth a try if you are ever feeling super adventurous. The success of this salad is due to romaine lettuce and crunchy croutons paired with a creamy dressing and then draped with cheese. But there's a secret star that you probably don't even know you're eating. Read the box below to see what that star is.

Prep: 20 minutes / Serves: 4

1 large head romaine lettuce, washed and drained dry

1 cup croutons (you can make these at home by baking cubes of bread tossed in oil at 325 degrees until crisp)

½ cup Caesar dressing

¼ cup Parmesan, grated

pepper

1 tin (2 ounces) anchovy fillets in oil, drained (optional)

① Slice the romaine lengthwise into three strips. Then cut the strips across to create bite-size pieces. Place them in a serving bowl and toss with the croutons. Drizzle the dressing evenly over the greens and sprinkle on the cheese.

② Grind some fresh black pepper onto the salad and then lay the anchovy fillets (if using) onto the salad and serve.

Small Fish Superstars

You might think you wouldn't touch anchovies with a 10-foot pole, but guess what? If you've ever eaten a Caesar salad before, chances are that you've gobbled them down. (Hint: They're hidden in the dressing!)

And the truth is, we should be eating a lot more anchovies *and* sardines, because they're good for you, and it's good for the environment. Small fish not only tend to contain less mercury (a harmful substance caused by ocean pollution), but also their small bones actually give us more calcium and add a great crunch. Plus, small fish are plentiful, so we can eat them without depleting them from our oceans. Win-win!

Delicious Fish in Tomato Sauce

Grilling weather not cooperating with you? That's okay! You can still enjoy a tasty seafood meal right on the stove top. You might be used to your fish fillets breaded and fried, but the sauce in this dish is so delicious you won't even miss the breaded coating! You can use just about any white fish fillet, but I recommend pollock or Pacific halibut. The better quality of fish, the better the dish, so you might want to ask the person at the store what's good that day.

Prep: 15 minutes / Cook: 10 minutes / Serves: 4

2 tablespoons olive oil

1 clove garlic, minced

2 teaspoons dried oregano

1 can (14 ounces) fire-roasted diced tomatoes

¼ cup water

1½ pound boneless, skinless white fish

salt

① In a large saute pan (big enough for all fillets to lie flat), heat the oil over medium heat and add the garlic. When the garlic begins to smell yummy, add the oregano and stir. Immediately add the tomatoes and the water. Stir to combine and bring to a simmer (so it's bubbling a little bit but not quite boiling).

② Season the fish generously with salt and add it to the pan.

③ Reduce the heat to low and cover the pan. Depending on how thick the fillets are, the fish should be cooked in about 7–10 minutes per inch of thickness.

④ To serve, carefully remove the fish from the pan and place on top of rice, whole wheat pasta, or another grain. Scoop out the tomato sauce and place on top of the fish. Serve immediately.

green scene

Ocean Alert!

It may seem as if the world's oceans are so vast that nothing could hurt them. Unfortunately, that's not true. The oceans suffer from people dumping stuff in them that they don't want (pollution) and taking too much from them that they do want (overfishing). You can help turn this problem around.

You probably already know how to help fight pollution: Participate in stream, river, and beach cleanups; don't litter; and don't dump things down storm drains. But you may not realize that too many fish—including the bluefin tuna shown here—are taken from the sea. Some overfished species, such as sharks, are disappearing.

People kill 100 million sharks every year. The desire for shark fin soup is one big reason so many sharks die. These fish are caught, their fins are cut off to be sold, and the rest of their bodies are thrown back into the sea.

Many fish are slow growing, and live decades or even centuries. Orange roughies can live to be more than 100. Rockfish can live to be 200! And Chilean seabass live 40 years. When there aren't enough of these slow-growing fish, it threatens the species because the fish often are taken from the sea before they are old enough to reproduce. These species could disappear.

Read on to learn more about the ocean and how you can help.

BE AN OCEAN HERO!

You can be part of the solution if you carefully choose what fish to eat. Some are okay to eat; others you should avoid because they're overfished or caught in ways that harm the ocean. This list is an example of the information available to guide our seafood choices. To get the most up-to-date info, check out our Seafood Decision Guide at *www.natgeoseafood.com*. Ask your parents to consult it when they buy fish at the market or order it at a restaurant. Ask the grocer or chef where and how the fish was caught. Saving marine life is hard, but if everyone helps, it will make a difference.

BEST CHOICES

abalone (farmed)
barramundi (U.S.)
catfish (U.S.)
caviar/sturgeon (farmed)
char, Arctic (farmed)
clams (farmed)
clams, softshell
crab, Dungeness
crab, stone
crawfish (U.S.)
halibut, Pacific
lobster, spiny
  (Australia, Baja, U.S.)
mackerel, Atlantic
mahimahi (U.S. troll)
mullet (U.S.)
mussels (farmed)
oysters (farmed)
pollock, Alaska

sablefish/black cod
  (Alaska, Canada)
salmon (Alaska wild)
salmon, canned
  pink/sockeye
sardines (U.S.)
scallops, bay (farmed)
shrimp, pink
  (Oregon)
shrimp (U.S. farmed)
spot prawn (Canada)
squid, longfin (U.S.)
striped bass (farmed)
tilapia (U.S.)
trout, rainbow (farmed)
tuna, albacore
  (Canada, U.S.)
tuna, yellowfin
  (U.S. troll)

WORST CHOICES

caviar/sturgeon (imported wild)
Chilean seabass
cod, Atlantic
crab, king
  (imported)
crawfish (China)
flounder/sole (Atlantic)
grouper
haddock (trawl)
halibut, Atlantic
mahimahi (imported longline)
monkfish
orange roughy

rockfish (Pacific trawl)
salmon (farmed or Atlantic)
shark
shrimp/prawns (imported)
skate
snapper (red or imported)
swordfish (imported)
tilapia (Asia)
tuna, bigeye
  (longline)
tuna, bluefin
tuna, yellowfin
  (imported longline)

June challenge

Protein Power-Up

So, chances are you've probably had an adult tell you that you need to eat more protein. Well, I hate to side with your parents on this one, but protein is a super important part of your diet—it fills you up so much better than that bag of potato chips or cupcake you've had your eye on. What exactly is protein?

In a nutshell, protein is the stuff that builds, maintains, and replaces the tissues in your body to keep you healthy, active, and feeling full. Lots of foods contain proteins, but the best sources are

meats (especially white meat or lean beef)

dairy

eggs

seafood

nuts and seeds

legumes (peanuts, beans)

processed soy products (like tofu and veggie burgers)

In the United States, we get most of our protein from meat, which is why this month's challenge is all about using a great variety of proteins to power up mealtimes. Each day, pick a meal and give it an extra protein boost from one of the categories listed above. Record your results on a separate sheet of paper. Write down each mealtime, list what you ate, and how you gave it a protein boost. Keep track of what you liked and what you didn't, so you know what you do and do not want to try again.

See if you can use your newfound protein prowess to add it where you least expect it—try apples with a slice of cheese for dessert, or make yourself a three-bean salad. At the end of the week, score yourself! Give yourself 1 point for each day you added an extra protein to your meal. Then give yourself a bonus point if you used a different type of protein each day. So what's your score? You're aiming for 10!

Cheese

Lentils

Tofu

Mixed Beans

Veggie Burger

Beef

Eggs

Milk

Pork Chops

Nuts

Salmon

Chicken

PEOPLE PROFILE

Dune Lankard

FISHERMAN:
Dune Lankard is a hero for conservation. He is also a fisherman. Dune was born in Alaska as a member of the Eyak tribe. Dune's relatives had fished the icy cold waters of Alaska for thousands of years before the *Exxon Valdez* oil tanker ran aground in 1989. His livelihood and heritage threatened by the oil spill, Dune became a leader in his community, pushing for measures that would preserve his tribe's ability to thrive off the land of his ancestors.

Forrest Pritchard

RANCHER:
Forrest Pritchard is a professional farmer in Virginia, where he tends to the farm that has been in his family for generations. Forrest, a shining example of a modern farmer, has endured many hard times in making his farm a profitable business. His success is largely due to his participation in local farmers markets, where he has made great quality products available to city folks and has created a loyal following of thousands of people who have been reconnected with the source of their food.

Plan a Picnic

Green Summer Adventures

Family Chef Competition

July, in many places, brings long, hot, lazy days. It's easy to blame soaring temperatures for making us seek the comfort of the indoors, but spend too much time inside and chances are your parents will urge you to "go outside and do something." Here's an idea: Grab your friends and have a picnic! Doing something out of the ordinary can often inspire a fresh outlook on life.

Just as it's fun to try new ingredients, it's also fun to try them in a new place. **Try the local park, the zoo, or even your backyard!**

plan a picnic

Planning a summer picnic menu is all about fresh, easy ingredients that are portable and don't require being served hot. You wouldn't want to rest under the shade of a tree and eat hot soup in 100-degree weather, would you? Here are a couple of easy ideas for a delicious warm-weather picnic.

Zesty Coleslaw

You may think of coleslaw as the stuff that goes on top of your barbecue. That's because it's most often just an afterthought to a meal. But it's actually a great side dish that goes with seemingly everything. When made with care and a little creativity, slaw can be a real treat all on its own. Here I use Greek yogurt instead of mayonnaise to make this a healthy and unexpected crowd-pleaser.

Prep: 30 minutes / Serves: 4

½ head green cabbage, thinly shredded

2 carrots, peeled and shredded

3 teaspoons salt

3 tablespoons apple cider vinegar

½ cup plain Greek yogurt

1 tablespoon onion powder

2 teaspoons celery seed

salt

1. In a large bowl, mix the cabbage with the carrot, salt, and vinegar. Toss to combine and let sit for at least 2 minutes, so the flavors combine.

2. Meanwhile, in a separate bowl, mix the yogurt, onion powder, and celery seed and whisk to blend into a dressing. Add the dressing to the cabbage mixture and toss to combine.

3. Check the seasoning and add more salt if necessary. Let sit for 15 minutes before serving.

plan a picnic

FETA IS ONE OF THE WORLD'S OLDEST CHEESES!

THE AVERAGE LIFE SPAN OF AN OLIVE TREE IS 500 YEARS.

TRY THIS! CREATE A PASTA SALAD THAT'S UNIQUE TO YOUR TASTES BY ADDING THINGS LIKE CHEDDAR CHEESE, GREEN PEPPERS, PEPPERONI, CARROTS, CUCUMBER, CORN, OR BLACK BEANS!

Crowd-Pleasing Pasta Salad

Orzo is a tiny, diamond-shape pasta that I can best describe as being fun to eat. In this salad I pair it with the tangy bite of feta cheese, the salty punch of olives, and the sweetness of cherry tomatoes. This is an easy dish to make in large quantities to eat over the course of a couple of days. It's also easy to swap out ingredients if you're not a fan of feta or olives. (But try it this way first. It's good—I promise!)

Prep: 30 minutes / Serves: 4

salt

1 pound orzo pasta

¼ cup olive oil

¼ cup feta cheese, crumbled

1 tablespoon chopped fresh oregano
(or ½ tablespoon dried oregano)

1 lemon, juiced

1 cup cherry tomatoes,
cut in quarters

¼ cup black, Greek, or green olives

1. Bring a large pot of salted water to a boil. Add the orzo and cook according to the instructions on the package, usually for about 8–12 minutes. Drain the pasta and place it into a large bowl.

2. Mix the orzo with the oil, feta, oregano, and lemon juice. Toss to combine.

3. Once the orzo is fully cooled, add the tomatoes and olives and stir to blend. Serve at room temperature.

EDIBLE WEATHER REPORT

Spanish settlers were growing watermelons in Florida by 1576!

Dutch farmers cultivate specially colored peppers that are available in brown, lilac, and deep purple.

Because kiwi fruit is so popular in New Zealand, New Zealanders are often called Kiwis!

Several Filipino dishes use unripe green papayas for flavor and texture.

Melons
FLORIDA & CALIFORNIA, U.S.A.

Bell Peppers
HOLLAND

Papaya
PHILIPPINES

Kiwi
NEW ZEALAND

Picnic-Perfect Chicken Salad

Chicken salad is a tried-and-true picnic classic. The cold chicken with the mix of creamy mayonnaise and spices is a refreshing summer treat. And before you shy away from adding fruit, give it a chance! The sweet crunch of grapes adds an unexpected but delicious surprise!

Prep: 1 hour / Serves: 4

1¼-pound chicken breast, boneless and skinless

water

4 tablespoons mayonnaise

2 tablespoons chopped fresh tarragon (or 3 tablespoons dried tarragon)

1 cup green or red seedless grapes, sliced in half

8 slices whole wheat toast

salt

① Place the chicken in a small pot just big enough to hold it. Fill the pot with cold water and place over medium heat. As soon as the water begins to bubble, reduce the heat to low and let cook for approximately 15 minutes, or until the chicken is cooked to 165 degrees measured with a meat thermometer. Remove from the heat and drain off the liquid.

② When the chicken is cooled, cut it into small pieces and place them in a bowl. Add the mayonnaise, tarragon, and grapes and stir to combine. Let the mixture sit for 10 minutes for the flavors to combine. Season to taste, serve on toasted bread and enjoy!

KITCHEN SKILL

Cleaning Up as You Go One of the worst parts of cooking is the cleanup, especially if you've let everything pile up for after the meal. Cleaning up as you go is a very important kitchen skill that will make your life so much easier in the long run. The best way to avoid the messy-kitchen aftermath is to wash your dishes during the cooking process. Whenever you dirty a pot, bowl, or utensil, immediately take it to the sink and wash it. It is a lot easier to wash 1 thing at a time than 25 things at a time. This way, you also help keep yourself organized. Organization is key to good cooking. If you are stressing out about finding tools or pans, it can be a real distraction. The cleaner your space is, the easier it is to focus on the task at hand.

IN THE NETHERLANDS, MAYONNAISE IS THE CONDIMENT OF CHOICE FOR FRENCH FRIES!

Green Summer Adventures

Summer is the best time to get out into nature with your picnic basket in hand. Why not turn that into a mission to save nature as well? The more we take care of our environment, the better it will be for us to enjoy. Try these easy ideas for a green summer.

WHAT TO DO

1 VISIT A NATIONAL PARK.
By visiting national parks in the United States as well as in other countries, you help encourage governments to save wild areas. Many animals—from bears to dolphins, zebras to manatees—depend on protected areas.

2 SHAKE IT UP.
Using products that are powered by shaking or winding (such as flashlights and radios) makes use of your energy, which is renewable, and helps keep batteries out of landfills.

3 BE A CUTUP.
If your family brings along beverages that come in a six-pack container with plastic rings, cut the rings apart to prevent animals from getting entangled in them. Many cities will even accept the plastic for recycling.

4 HELP WILDLIFE STAY WILD.
Whether you are spending a day at the beach or taking a hike in the mountains, be sure to leave wild animals alone. Each time someone takes a sea star out of its habitat or feeds a deer, an ecosystem is upset and natural behaviors are disturbed.

5 CONSERVE CLEAN CLOTHES.
Instead of changing your clothes several times a day, think about your schedule ahead of time and pick the right outfit for the entire day. If you do one less load of laundry a week, you can save as much as 2,000 gallons of water a year.

IN THE COMPETITIVE WORLD OF SAND SCULPTING, PEOPLE MAKE DRAGONS, MERMAIDS, AND EVEN REPLICAS OF REAL CASTLES OUT OF SAND!

Family Chef Competition

July can be one of the most exhilarating months of all, but sometimes too much heat and free time can also lead to boredom ... and one too many reality TV shows! This month, star in your own reality show by hosting the Family Chef Competition. You get to bust boredom *and* school your family at the same time!

1 Start the competition by choosing one family member to be the judge (or invite a friend to judge). Have the judge pick 3–5 healthy "mystery" ingredients.

2 If you have time, the judge can remove or cover labels to make the "reveal" extra interesting. Or, he or she can write down the ingredient list and deliver it to each chef to find in the pantry or refrigerator. When the reveal is made, each cook has 30 minutes to create the best meal using all of those foods. Of course, you can allow chefs to supplement the mystery ingredients with other foods from the kitchen, otherwise you might end up with similar dishes.

3 After the 30 minutes are up, the judge chooses the winner based on taste and creativity!

TRY THIS! TO MAKE THE COMPETITION EVEN MORE CHALLENGING, THE JUDGE CAN ASSIGN FOOD CATEGORIES (SUCH AS APPETIZER, MAIN COURSE, OR DESSERT) AHEAD OF TIME. MAKE SURE TO PICK AN AWESOME PRIZE FOR THE WINNER!

Goin' Veggie

Has anyone ever told you that they are vegetarian, and you've wondered exactly what that meant? Vegetarians eat an entirely plant-based diet. This is a choice people make for a number of reasons—for some, it's health reasons, for others it's personal beliefs. Many of the foods that are most healthy for us are plant-based. Many people recognize that the meat production process also contributes to pollution and climate change more so than producing plant-based foods. Other people reject the idea of eating animals.

Whatever the reasoning, there are many ways to enjoy a diet that is rich in plant-based foods. If you are not vegetarian, but are concerned about the impact that eating meat has on the world, you could go veggie one or two days a week and gain some of the health and environmental benefits. Many of the dishes that we already love so much—like pasta, pizza, soup, and salad—can be made vegetarian quite easily. Try "Meatless Mondays" for a few weeks and see if it works for you!

Heritage Recipes

Water, Water Everywhere!

Family Recipe Book

August is a month for family. It was always when Mom and Dad would take time off work, camp would end, and the days were all ours. We would usually take a trip to visit my grandparents, and I remember those times very fondly. The food was always the best part. Traditional recipes that had been perfected over decades would be served. It was food that was comforting and made me feel as though I was right where I belonged. The dishes were simple, but they told my family history. **It was through these meals that I learned a lot about myself.**

heritage recipes

PEOPLE HAVE BEEN EATING PICKLES SINCE THE MESOPOTAMIANS BEGAN MAKING THEM IN 2400 B.C.!

Not-So-Sloppy Joes

I remember very well going to my great-aunt Shirley's house for a couple of days each summer. She had a knack for traditional "kid food," and her meatloaf and sloppy joes were the highlight of the trip. Even as an adult, I re-create her recipes, and this sloppy joe is always a crowd-pleaser. To my mind, a good sloppy joe isn't *too* sloppy. In this recipe I try to keep the filling a little thicker so that you only need 1 napkin—instead of 10—to keep yourself clean. You'll be happy, and so will whoever is doing the cleanup!

Prep: 10 minutes / Cook: 35 minutes / Serves: 4

1 pound ground beef (10–20% fat)

1 yellow onion, peeled and diced

1 tablespoon dried oregano

1 tablespoon Worcestershire sauce

1 tablespoon red wine vinegar

1 can (6 ounces) tomato paste

1½ cups tomato sauce

salt

4 whole wheat hamburger buns

1. In a large sauté pan, break up the beef into small chunks and cook over medium heat, stirring frequently until it begins to release some of its fat and juices.

2. Add the onion and stir to mix well. Cook over medium heat for another 10 minutes, or until the onion begins to soften.

3. Add the oregano, Worcestershire sauce, vinegar, and tomato paste. Stir to combine and cook for 5 minutes while stirring constantly. Add the tomato sauce and season with salt. Stir to combine.

4. Turn the heat to low. Cover the pot and simmer for 15 minutes. Toast the hamburger buns. Scoop the beef mixture onto the buns and serve.

heritage
recipes

Understanding Heritage

The word "heritage" means something that is passed from one person or thing to another. In this sense, your family heritage is all the customs, traditions, and yes, recipes, that your family passes down from one generation to the next. It is often rooted deeply in your family's history and may include customs from the countries of origin of your grandparents, great-grandparents, and so on. Because of all the different people who have come together in your family's past, heritage recipes are unique. They may combine the flavors and traditions of different countries. For instance, you may visit your mom's family and eat spaghetti from their native country of Italy. Then you may head to your dad's family to feast on salsa from Mexico. The cool part is that you could combine your mom's Italian heritage with your dad's Mexican heritage to create a "salsa spaghetti" recipe that you can pass on to your kids one day!

MANY PEOPLE RESEARCH THEIR ANCESTRY AND CREATE FAMILY TREES IN A PROCESS CALLED GENEALOGY.

Grandma's Potato Salad

There are as many styles of potato salad as there are cooks. This one is made in the style of what my grandmother used to cook for us when we were visiting her.

Prep: 20 minutes /
Cook: 15 minutes / Serves: 4

1 pound red potatoes

salt

¾ cup mayonnaise
(or plain Greek yogurt)

1 lemon, juiced

1 tablespoon whole grain mustard

1 tablespoon onion powder

2 teaspoons celery seed

½ cup fresh dill sprigs
(or 2 tablespoons dried dill)

 1 Place the potatoes in a pot and cover with cold water. Season generously with salt and place on the stove over high heat.

 2 As the water begins to boil, reduce the heat to medium and cook for 10–15 minutes, or until the potatoes are soft and just beginning to fall apart (you should be able to easily stab them with a fork). Drain and let the potatoes cool.

3 Meanwhile, mix the remaining ingredients with a whisk until combined.

4 When the potatoes are cool enough to handle, gently mash them with a spoon until you have large chunks, and then add the mayonnaise dressing.

 5 Toss to combine and adjust the seasoning with more salt if necessary. Allow to sit for at least 10 minutes for the flavors to come together. Serve at room temperature.

Refrigerator Pickles

With this recipe, you can enjoy pickle-y goodness in just 24 hours. But they do get better with age, so you might want to give them a few days for the flavors to really combine. These will last a couple of weeks in the fridge.

Prep: 20 minutes / Chill: At least 1 day / Makes: 1 quart

1 empty and sterilized quart jar
(You can sterilize a jar by boiling it in water. Ask a parent for help if you don't have a sterile jar on hand.)

½ cup water

½ cup apple cider vinegar

½ yellow onion, peeled and thinly sliced

3 allspice berries (optional)

3 cloves (optional)

1 teaspoon fennel seeds

1 tablespoon salt

4–6 small cucumbers, sliced in half lengthwise

1 Combine all the ingredients except the cucumbers in a saucepan and bring to a boil. Meanwhile, place the cucumber halves into the jar, jamming them in as best as you can.

2 When the vinegar mixture reaches a boil, get a parent to *very* carefully pour it into the jar with cucumbers, filling it up to the very top.

3 Cover the jar with the lid and allow to cool to room temperature on the counter. Once it has cooled, place the jar in the fridge and wait at least 1 day. Ta-da! You now have refrigerator pickles!

TRY THIS! THERE ARE MANY PICKLING VARIATIONS. YOU CAN SUBSTITUTE SPICES IF YOU WISH, ADD SUGAR FOR A SWEETER PICKLE, OR EVEN ADD SOME CHILI PEPPERS TO GIVE THE PICKLES A NICE KICK.

When it comes to heritage recipes,

pickles (and pickled vegetables) are a dime a dozen. That's because back in the olden days, before modern means of maintaining and growing vegetation year-round, people had to figure out a way to preserve their produce. Pickling was common because it is cheap and super easy. However, it can take a long time. Traditional pickles need to sit on the shelf for weeks or even months before they are ready. Refrigerator pickles are not meant for long-term storage. Rather than preserving, you are really just adding flavor to give your meal some character.

 **CHEW ON THIS**

CUCUMBERS are actually fruit. They are in the same family as cantaloupe!

There's an entire museum devoted to **VINEGAR** in Roslyn, South Dakota.

In ancient times, **SALT** was so valuable it was used as currency.

The Truth About Food Waste

Each day, every day, we waste a lot of food. In our daily lives, it may not seem like a big deal. Sometimes it's because we don't really want to finish the carrots that were served to us. Other times we don't cook ingredients before they go bad. And because we have a tendency to want to eat an apple only if it's perfectly round and red, we waste food in the fields just because it doesn't look appetizing enough. About 50 percent of all the food that is produced globally is wasted. But you can make a difference. By shopping at a local farmers market, you can encourage farmers to bring to market all of their produce, not just the perfect stuff. You can even pick out the ugly apples that you think others might leave behind. You have a lot more power than you think, and if more people change their attitudes about food, it would make a huge impact!

green scene

Water, Water Everywhere!

Water is the most essential ingredient in food and cooking. Not only do we use water to cook ingredients, such as when steaming broccoli or boiling potatoes, but also water makes up the majority of many of the foods we eat. Ever wonder why a watermelon is called a watermelon? Well, that's because it's more than 90 percent water. So is broccoli. In fact, most plants are mostly water. But water runs even deeper in our food. One pound of beef requires almost 1,800 gallons of water to produce. This water is given directly to the cow and is used to irrigate the feed and in processing. No food can grow without water, and lack of fresh water is one of the main limiting factors surrounding food production. So what can you do to help?

WHAT TO DO

1 Turn off the faucet while you are brushing your teeth.

2 Take short showers instead of baths.

3 Make sure your parents fix any leaky faucets or toilets.

4 Above all, realize how important water is to your life and use it responsibly.

ONLY 3 PERCENT OF EARTH'S WATER IS FRESH WATER.

1.7 PERCENT OF THE WORLD'S WATER IS FROZEN, AND THEREFORE UNUSABLE.

Sandra Postel

Sandra Postel is a National Geographic explorer who has dedicated her career to conservation of water resources. She travels all over the planet sharing innovative techniques for reducing water usage. She also educates people on why water is so important and its conservation essential to human health and well-being. In 1994, Sandra founded the Global Water Policy Project to help promote the preservation and sustainable use of Earth's freshwater resources. She has also authored several books on water conservation and the importance of sustainability. She says, "I love nature—and water is the source of it all. I care about the mussels and fish and frogs that depend on water. The extinction of life pains me. I just want to do my part to be sure we humans conserve water and share it with all of life."

challenge

Family Recipe Book

August is a great time for family reunions. The sun is shining, school is still out, and families can come together to re-create all sorts of traditions. For many families, that means cooking together! Take advantage of your together time by creating a family cookbook. Ask relatives and close family friends for their favorite recipes and then compile them in a beautiful keepsake cookbook. Use markers, ribbons, or other materials to decorate the book however you'd like.

Make the book extra special by writing down treasured memories alongside the recipes. Ask easy questions like "Who taught you how to cook?" or "What is your favorite memory of a meal?"

Now for the challenge: Try to re-create all the recipes! Which ones do you like? How are they different from each other? If you want, pick your favorite recipe once you have tried them all and give the winner a signed copy of your cookbook!

THERE IS NO ONE WAY TO MAKE A HOMEMADE COOKBOOK. You can buy an album from a store and fill it in, create your own, or even hire a printing company to print one up for you. Here's an easy way to make one at home!

SUPPLIES

- family recipes
- construction paper
- glue
- decorating materials such as markers, ribbons, glitter, photos, stickers, etc.
- treasured memories
- clear page protectors (optional)
- binder (optional)
- 3-hole punch

1. Type up or write out the recipes you've collected from your family and friends (if they wrote them out for you, you can use the originals).

2. Organize your recipes. You can separate them into sections by meal course, food type, family member, or whatever makes sense.

3. Firmly glue each recipe to a piece of construction paper.

4. Decorate each page any way you'd like! Try adding treasured memories near each recipe.

5. If you want, you can slip each page inside a clear, plastic page protector. If you're using a binder or pre-made album, add your pages in. Otherwise, neatly line up all your pages and use your 3-hole punch on your recipes. You can then bind the construction papers into a book using pretty ribbon. Don't forget to decorate the cover and give your book a title!

Lunch!

Scheduling September

Pack Your Lunch!

September is the month when we reorganize our lives into schedules. With the hot, hazy days of summer slipping away, it's time to get back to work (or homework!). But just because the neighborhood pool is closing, it doesn't mean the fun has to end. Think of it more as a clean slate: new backpack, new school supplies, and a new attitude toward life. September is a great time to practice what you've learned while cooking over the summer. **Plan a few lunches and amaze your friends with what you create!**

lunch!

Face it. Between science and social studies, English and extracurriculars, the school day, can get a little—well—long. But there's one bright shining beacon of freedom every day that keeps you chugging along till it's time to hit the bus: lunch.

Lunchtime is your time. The cafeteria should be your sanctuary. But sometimes lunch can fall into a routine. Here are a few of my favorite ideas for sprucing up a boring box or bag:

Salmon Salad Sandwich

Before you go running for the hills after reading the name of this dish, consider this: You've eaten tuna salad before, right? Most types of salmon are very sustainable, which means what we take from the oceans is plentiful and doesn't impact the environment in harmful ways (see the chart on page 79 for more information on choosing what fish to eat). A fun challenge is to try a salmon sandwich right next to a tuna sandwich and see if you taste a big difference. Me? I actually prefer the salmon.

Prep: 20 minutes / Serves: 4

1 can (15 ounces) boneless, skinless pink or red salmon

2 tablespoons mayonnaise

½ tablespoon onion powder

1 tablespoon pickle relish (or chopped dill pickle)

juice of ½ lemon

1 teaspoon celery salt

8 slices whole wheat bread, toasted

1 Open and drain the can of salmon. Mix the mayonnaise, onion powder, relish, lemon juice, and celery salt in a bowl. Whisk to combine.

2 Add the salmon to the mayonnaise mixture and, using two forks, gently mix until well combined, taking care not to break up the chunks of salmon too much.

3 When well incorporated, scoop the salmon onto the bread and spread it flat. Garnish with your favorite ingredients, such as thinly sliced cucumber, lettuce, and tomato, and, if you're like me, slather it with hot sauce!

lunch!

Anatomy of a Sandwich

All sandwiches are not created equal. Have you ever had turkey on soggy wheat bread, or roast beef on rye that just won't hold together? You can avoid these issues with just a little effort ahead of time. For example, tomatoes release a lot of moisture, so if you are using tomato slices on a sandwich, make sure to put them in the middle of the stack of ingredients to keep them away from the bread. If you are using hummus or mayonnaise, put half of it on each slice of bread, thus reducing the chance that it will squeeze out when you take a bite. If you are using lettuce or spinach, tear it into pieces before putting it on the sandwich. That way you won't pull out the whole leaf on the first bite and pull the sandwich apart with it! Each sandwich should be just as fun and unique as the person who makes it. Follow these simple steps to foolproof your favorites:

Place two slices of bread (toasted or untoasted, depending on your preference) on a cutting board.

Add a thin smear of your favorite condiment to each side of the bread (so too much of a good thing doesn't squeeze out the sides).

Add dry veggies (such as spinach or lettuce), cut into small strips or chunks, to both sides of the main ingredient. This will protect your bread and prevent it from getting soggy. You can also include cheese in your "protective layer."

Add moist veggies (like tomatoes and cucumbers) on top of the dry layer.

Add the main ingredient (such as turkey, veggies, or ham) so that it falls right in the center of the sandwich.

BONUS TIP: If you are enjoying a peanut butter and jelly sandwich for lunch, put a small amount of peanut butter on both pieces of the bread with your jelly layer on top of that. This will prevent the jelly from leaking through your sandwich.

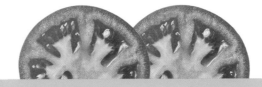

Ham and Roasted Veggie Sandwich

I love the taste of thinly sliced vegetables that have been grilled or roasted, chilled, and served the next day. The flavors have had time to come together, and they can liven up any boring old dish! In this sandwich you can let your imagination run wild by using nearly any combination of ingredients. I really like to use hummus as a condiment—it adds richness and flavor without the fat of mayonnaise (see "Sandwich Swaps" below).

Prep: 20 minutes / Cook: 40 minutes /
Serves: 2–3

1 large zucchini

1 large yellow squash

1 tablespoon olive oil

salt

4–6 slices whole grain bread, toasted

2 tablespoons mayonnaise or hummus

2 large leaves of lettuce, shredded

6 ounces sliced deli ham

1 For the vegetables, preheat your oven to 400 degrees. Carefully slice the zucchini and squash into ½-inch-thick slices.

2 Toss the slices with the olive oil and salt. Place the veggies in a baking dish and put it into the oven.

3 When the vegetables are just beginning to color and have become soft, after about 40 minutes, remove them from the oven and let them cool.

4 For the sandwich, spread the bread with mayonnaise or hummus. Stack the roasted vegetables and the lettuce on top, then fold over a slice of ham.

Sandwich Swaps

Sandwiches are an ever present feature of the school lunch box. The ease of putting the ingredients together, on top of the portability factor, just can't be beat. But if you're bored with what's between your bread, shake things up a little. There is an amazing amount of options to try when it comes to the humble hoagie. Here are a couple of my favorites:

INSTEAD OF ...	TRY ...
mayonnaise	guacamole, hummus, mustard
jelly	fresh sliced fruit, a drizzle of honey
lettuce	spinach, thinly sliced cucumber, sliced radish
cheese	avocado slices, roasted red pepper, sun-dried tomato

scheduling

Homework, soccer practice, dog walking ... busy lives require a little planning, especially when it comes to dinner! It can be hard to find time to cook when take-out food is so convenient. The answer? Make cooking at home just as convenient by planning ahead. You can cook big batches of basic food bases and then use them in different ways throughout the week. This can be done with all sorts of foods (think beans, broth, and boiled eggs), so it's easy to do the work just once and enjoy the convenience throughout the week. Check out this recipe for simple quinoa, which you can flavor with just about anything.

Simple Quinoa

Traditionally grown in countries like Bolivia, Peru, and Ecuador, quinoa is a superfood that has sustained many cultures for hundreds of years. Today, this nutrient-packed and delicious staple has become the darling food of health-conscious eaters and top chefs alike. It is important to wash quinoa very thoroughly before cooking, as a bitter powder residue often covers the seeds. Once you do that, the result will be a sweet, nutty, and fluffy dish.

Prep: 5 minutes / Cook: 20 minutes / Serves: 4

2 tablespoons olive oil   4 cups water

2 cups quinoa, washed   salt
and dried

1 In a large pot, heat the oil over high heat. Add the quinoa and stir constantly to toast the grains.

2 Just as the quinoa begins to color slightly, add the water and reduce the heat to low. Season with salt and cover the pot. Cook for about 20 minutes and then fluff the quinoa with a fork.

3 If there is any remaining water in the pot, then remove the lid and continue to cook until it has all been absorbed. Add salt to taste. Serve immediately or chill and use for any number of dishes (such as in salads or in place of rice)!

TRY THIS MONDAY! QUINOA FOR BREAKFAST: TOSS IN SOME FRESH FRUIT, PECANS, A LITTLE CINNAMON, AND MAYBE EVEN SOME HONEY OR MAPLE SYRUP.

TRY THIS TUESDAY! ADD SOME CHOPPED CUCUMBERS, TOMATOES, ONIONS, OIL, GARLIC, AND SEASONINGS TO CREATE A MIDDLE EASTERN QUINOA SALAD.

TRY THIS WEDNESDAY! THROW SOME QUINOA INTO A PAN AND SAUTÉ IT WITH VEGGIES AND A LITTLE BIT OF SOY SAUCE OR COOKING OIL.

PEOPLE PROFILE

Alice Waters

Alice Waters is a visionary chef who founded a restaurant called Chez Panisse (shay pah-neese). There, she revolutionized American food by reintroducing us to fresh vegetables picked at the peak of flavor and presented simply. Her cooking has inspired generations of chefs who have made fresh flavor the centerpiece of American food. Alice also started another delicious revolution when she founded the Edible Schoolyard Project, an organization dedicated to improving the quality of food served at schools. The Edible Schoolyard Project also uses food to help educate students in the classroom, bringing the knowledge of food into the academic setting. By teaching kids to be fluent in food—knowing what different vegetables look like, for example—this organization seeks to create a healthy generation in which people treat themselves and the planet with care and respect.

green scene

Make a Reusable Lunch Bag

Did you know that the average kid ages 8 to 12 throws away about 67 pounds of lunch waste each year? That's about the same weight as an average eight-year-old boy! So before you chow down, make sure your lunch is garbage-free. By packing only what you can eat, reuse, or recycle, you will reduce the amount of waste you contribute to landfills. Start creating a waste-free lunch by ditching the brown paper bag and making your own reusable lunch bag.

Buy snacks in large packages instead of individually wrapped ones. You will cut down on the amount of plastic packaging that ends up in landfills.

Put your food in reusable containers.

Drink from a Thermos instead of a disposable juice box.

Swap plastic tableware for a reusable set.

YOU WILL NEED

a parent's permission

old pair of jeans

scissors

needle and thread, or sewing machine

ribbon or cord

buttons, patches, or other items for decoration

WHAT TO DO

1 Cut a 14- to 16-inch section from one of the pant legs.

2 Fold a ½-inch strip around the top to create a place to string a cord. Sew it down, making sure to leave a small opening at both ends.

3 Thread a 3-foot length of ribbon or cord through the opening at the top to make a drawstring.

4 Cut an additional piece of fabric about 1 inch larger than the leg hole to create the bottom of the bag.

5 Turn the fabric inside out and sew the two sections together at the bottom.

6 Decorate the lunch bag with things from around your house, such as buttons and patches.

Share Your Food

One of the great joys of food is that we get to share it with those we love. Family dinners are the perfect time to come together and share stories of our busy days along with our food. The same idea can apply to lunchtime! Invite a few friends over on a weekend and ask everyone to bring a dish to share. When you share your food, talk about how you made it and maybe even tell a story about the dish and where it came from. You'll be surprised how much you can learn about someone by asking him or her about their food.

challenge

Pack
Your Lunch!

Sure, your sandwich might be the star of the show when it comes to DIY (do-it-yourself) lunches, but the supporting cast is just as important in preparing a well-rounded meal that will get you to 3:30 p.m. without fainting from hunger. So, September's challenge is to pack a tasty lunch that will power you up and keep you going, all while making your lunch-table buddies drool with jealousy. There are four key ingredients to a quality brown bag lunch:

1. The main ingredient
2. The crunch factor
3. The sweet side
4. The healthy habit

THE MAIN INGREDIENT: The point of the main is that you want some sort of base (be it bread or something else) that serves as a vehicle for delicious and nutritious proteins and produce. This is where that much-talked-about sandwich comes into play. If you've followed the tips in this chapter, your sandwich will steal the spotlight! But if sandwiches aren't your thing, never fear—salads and whole grain pastas with delicious greens and protein add-ins are great go-to ideas.

THE CRUNCH FACTOR: Sure, those individual bags of chips might seem appealing, but greasy fried potatoes don't really add a lot of staying power to your midday meal. Instead try a salty crunch that will pack a punch. Trail mix, nuts, veggies and dip, or even cheese and crackers are great on-the-go munchies, and they're guaranteed to keep your belly from rumbling before that bell rings.

THE SWEET SIDE: It's human nature to crave a little sugar on the side of your meal. But those prepackaged waxy chocolate cakes will have you in the dentist's chair before you can say "sweet." Instead, try yogurt (see the Raspberry Yogurt Parfait on page 30), granola, sugar-free pudding, fruit, or get weird with wiggly Jell-O. If you absolutely can't live without chocolate, go for a small chunk of dark chocolate. It has proven health benefits, and a little bit goes a long way.

THE HEALTHY HABIT: If you didn't work fruit and veggies into one of the two categories above, you'll want to make sure you round out your meal with something that will make your mom smile. Apples and bananas are easy, and they already come in their own handy prepackaged containers. There's no reason not to throw one in. Baby carrots, celery, and cucumber are also an easy addition.

Now that you know the basics, test yourself by grading the lunches in the pictures below.

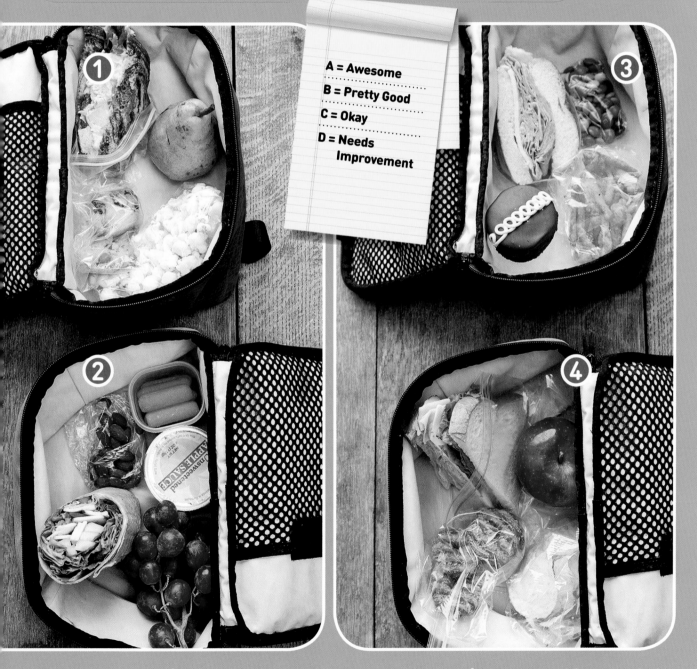

A = Awesome

B = Pretty Good

C = Okay

D = Needs Improvement

Next time you make your own lunch, give yourself a grade!
See our grades for these lunches on page 154.

Spooky Pizza Party

Edible Weather Report

Witches' Toenail Trail Mix

October is a fun month, chock-full of apple cider and pumpkins, hayrides, and bonfires. Your family has settled into their fall routine, and the rush of the holidays is not yet making your parents crazy. The nights may have a chill in the air, and we're all excited for Halloween. But as you are dressing up as a skeleton, ballerina, or zombie, nature is dressing up too! Summer colors turn to bright red, orange, and yellow, much like the foods of fall. Food is a great way to mark the passing of the seasons, and **fall is certainly putting on a show!**

Halloween is a busy night. You not only have to get into costume, but you also have to hit the streets before all the good candy is gone. So, what better quick meal to share with family and friends than pizza? Pizza is not just for delivery, and it doesn't have to come from the freezer either. Fresh pizza, made from delicious ingredients, is fun and easy to prepare. It all starts with the sauce. Once you have that done, the party can begin. Invite your friends over for a pre-trick-or-treat party, and have a blast making personal pizzas with all sorts of fun toppings.

Yummy Pizza Sauce

Good sauce is the key to a good pizza, so it makes sense to invest a little time into making something that really stands out. But keep in mind that people like their pizza sauce with all sorts of variations. So while my recipe might not be your yummy sauce, feel free to play around with the ingredients until you find the recipe that is right for you.

Prep: 10 minutes / Makes: Enough for 4 personal pizzas

2 cups pasta sauce (look for a smooth puree with not too many additional flavors)

1 can (6 ounces) tomato paste

½ tablespoon garlic powder

½ tablespoon onion powder

1 tablespoon dried oregano

Mix all the ingredients in a bowl and whisk to incorporate, making sure that there are no remaining lumps of tomato paste. It's as simple as that! Now turn the page and let the fun begin!

spooky
pizza
party

Jack-o'-Lantern
Personal Pita Pizzas

This is a fun way to dress up an everyday meal. Who says it's not okay to play with your food—especially when you're the one cooking it! Challenge your friends to see who can make the spookiest jack-o'-lantern face.

Prep: 15 minutes / Cook: 10 minutes / Serves: 4

4 10-inch whole wheat pita breads

1 cup Yummy Pizza Sauce (see page 121)

8 ounces grated cheese (provolone, mozzarella, or a blend work fine)

Toppings of your choice

Toppings checklist:

☐ Sliced mushrooms (button, shiitake, or portobello)

☐ Roasted or raw peppers

☐ Zucchini or yellow squash (cut into very thin half moons)

☐ Olives

☐ Fresh tomatoes (I really like cherry tomatoes, which explode in your mouth!)

☐ Green onions or scallions (finely shredded for "hair")

☐ Asparagus

☐ Artichoke hearts (these make great dimples on your pizza face)

☐ Spinach (if you want your jack-o'-lantern to have a 'fro)

☐ Onion (just be forewarned: red onions lose their color when they cook, and might look like worms, which might make them a perfect Halloween ingredient)

☐ Pepperoni (keep circular or cut into triangles for eyes)

☐ Anchovies (Yes, I said it. They are delicious, and what better occasion to try something that scares you?)

1 Preheat your oven to 450 degrees. Place the pitas on a baking tray. Spread a good amount (about ¼ cup) of the pizza sauce on each pita, leaving about a ½-inch crust. Sprinkle the cheese over the sauce.

2 Decorate your pizza with your jack-o'-lantern face and take a picture of the pizza before baking it. Place the tray in the hot oven and watch it cook, waiting until the cheese is melted and bubbly, about 7–10 minutes.

3 Remove it from the oven and take another picture so that you have a before and after shot! Carefully cut the pizza into pieces and enjoy. Any remaining sauce can be used as a dipping sauce for the "crust."

ACCORDING TO HIEROGLYPHICS, ANCIENT EGYPTIANS BELIEVED THAT MUSHROOMS WERE THE PLANT OF IMMORTALITY.

SOME FAVORITE PIZZA TOPPINGS IN JAPAN ARE SQUID, EEL, AND MAYO JAGA (MAYONNAISE, POTATO, AND BACON).

Ghoulish
Guacamole

If you're going to throw a spooky party, you need more than one creepy treat. Guacamole, made with mashed ripe avocados, is perfect for Halloween. It tastes delicious, but, let's face it, looks like a clump of green goo. Still, that doesn't stop it from being a party favorite. This tasty treat is simple to make, but there are a couple secrets to great guac that you need to know.

Buy good avocados. When shopping for these delicate fruits, you want to find ones that are just barely soft to the touch. Don't go squeezing every avocado, as you will bruise them and ruin them for other shoppers—just a very gentle amount of pressure will tell you whether they are ready to eat. They will also have a dark-green-bordering-on-black color.

Start blending with lime juice. When blending your guacamole, start with lime juice and marinate your ingredients in that before adding the avocado.

Prep: 15 minutes / Serves: 4

1–2 limes, juiced (depending on size and how much juice they have)

6 green onions or scallions, sliced very thin

1 small serrano or jalapeño chili, minced or grated (optional)

¼ cup cilantro, washed very well and finely chopped

salt (start with ½ teaspoon)

2–3 large ripe avocados

1. In a bowl, mix the lime juice with the scallion or green onion, chili pepper (if using), cilantro, and salt. Stir to combine and let sit for a few minutes while you prepare the avocados. When grating or cutting the chili pepper be very careful to wash your hands *very* thoroughly afterward as the spice will get into your eyes and skin if you touch them. It is also important to remove the seeds from the pepper (that's where most of the spice comes from).

2. Carefully use a small knife to cut each avocado lengthwise down to the pit and then turn the fruit around the blade to make a clean and even cut. Separate the two halves. Ask a parent to help remove the pit with the heel of a larger knife. Then slice the avocado with a butter knife while still in the shell in a crisscross pattern (this means less mashing later on).

3. Using a spoon, scrape the avocados out of the shell, scooping all the way down to the skin. Add them to the lime mixture and, using a whisk, mash them into the other ingredients until the texture is how you like it. Check the seasoning and adjust with more salt and lime juice if necessary. Serve immediately with fresh vegetables or tortilla chips.

BONUS TIP
WHEN STORING UNUSED GUACAMOLE, IT IS IMPORTANT THAT IT IS COVERED. AVOCADOS TURN BROWN VERY QUICKLY WHEN EXPOSED TO OXYGEN. THE SOLUTION IS TO PUT A PIECE OF PLASTIC WRAP DIRECTLY ON THE SURFACE OF THE REMAINING GUACAMOLE SO THAT IT HAS NO CONTACT WITH THE AIR. KEEP ANY LEFTOVERS REFRIGERATED.

IN SOME COUNTRIES, AVOCADOS ARE EATEN WITH ICE CREAM, OR BLENDED WITH MILK AND SUGAR FOR A SWEET DRINK.

EDIBLE WEATHER REPORT

America's oldest grapevine, called the Mother Vine, is around 400 years old.

Chile is the biggest blueberry producer in South America and the largest exporter to the Northern Hemisphere.

In Brazil, banana plant fiber is sometimes used to make clothing and accessories.

In the Balkans, apple pie is made with phyllo dough, a pastry made of many thin and flakey layers.

Grapes
CALIFORNIA
& NEW YORK,
U.S.A.

Apples
THE BALKANS

Bananas
BRAZIL

Berries
CHILE

scary snacks

Roasted Eyeball and Brains Bruschetta
(Grape and Cheese)

To round out your horrible holiday snacks, this treat combines wonderful flavors that can be paired and eaten on little pieces of toast. You probably know bruschetta as a bread and tomato dish, but in this version, I like to warm fresh grapes (eyeballs) until they burst and then combine them with cheese (brains) to serve over nutty bread. If blue cheese isn't your thing, you can also use cheddar, goat cheese, or another cheesy favorite.

Prep: 10 minutes / Cook: 10 minutes / Serves: 4

1 tablespoon olive oil

2 cups red grapes removed from the stem (wash and dry thoroughly—they will spatter when you add them if they are wet)

½ cup crumbled blue cheese (or any cheese of your choice)

4 slices whole grain and nut bread

1. In a small sauté pan, heat the oil over medium-high heat. Carefully add the grapes and allow to cook until they begin to split their skins and release their juice.

2. Give the pan one careful shake. As soon as the grapes begin to simmer in their own juices, about 3 minutes, remove from the heat and allow to sit in the pan for another 3 minutes so that they can heat all the way through (but be careful not to turn them to mush).

3. Meanwhile, toast the bread until it is crispy. Spoon the grapes over the pieces of toast and then crumble the cheese on top. Cut each piece of toast into 4 strips and serve warm.

JACK-O'-LANTERNS WERE MADE FROM TURNIPS UNTIL THE MID-1800s.

THERE ARE MORE THAN 8,000 VARIETIES OF GRAPES AROUND THE WORLD.

challenge

Witches' Toenail
Trail Mix

Okay, so trail mix doesn't actually contain witches' toenails (unless you want it to ... I suppose), but some beautiful things about this snack are that it's healthy, it's delicious, and you can make it with any number of things at any time of the year!

October is a great month for trail mix because it's a great snack-on-the-go for bike rides, camping trips, or hikes, and it's a snap to make. For this month's challenge, head on over to the bulk aisle of your grocery store and let your creativity lead you. The bulk aisle is where you'll find bins full of nuts, dried fruit, granola, seeds, and so much more. Your task is to build a mix that will energize and sustain you for hours and that strikes the right balance of tasty and satisfying. Here are a couple of secrets:

1 Don't go overboard and buy too much of one ingredient. Each bite should be a blend of flavors—not just your favorite flavor with a few flakes of granola so your mom approves.

2 Sweet and salty makes a great flavor combination. Don't be afraid to cover yet-uncharted flavor territory.

3 Dried fruit is sweet—really sweet—so don't make the mistake of adding unnecessary candy and sugar.

Trail Mix

There's no set recipe for trail mix, so instead I list a couple of options that I think blend well together. Don't be afraid to use more than one of the ingredients below, but just be sure not to overwhelm your mix.

1 Start with a base ingredient such as granola or flax clusters.

2 Add to this your choice of sweet, such as dried cranberries, dried bananas, dried apricots (cut into small pieces), and raisins.

3 Next, venture into the salty territory, with things like pumpkin seeds, almonds, walnuts, sesame seeds, and pecans.

4 Mix it all together with a big spoon and enjoy!

Now here's where the challenge comes in—let's call it an experiment on your family.

1 Once you find your favorite combination, put it in a clear container and make sure it's clearly marked in plain sight in the pantry or cupboard. Next, observe your family and make note of their snacking habits. Do they try your trail mix? Or do they head straight for the potato chips? Track them for a week and see how often they make the healthy decision.

2 For the second week, make it easier for them to grab your mix on the go. Scoop it into individual baggies that can be easily thrown in a backpack or briefcase. Move the unhealthy snacks farther out of reach. Does it change their habits at all?

3 Once you have gathered and recorded your evidence, present your findings to your family. Are they surprised? Do you think it will cause them to think more about healthy eating habits in the future?

NOV

Harvest Feast

Create a Green Thanksgiving

Leftovers Bonanza

November is a unique month. It is not often that our attention is fully turned to a meal. While many countries have a celebration in which they give thanks and enjoy the fruits of the harvest, Americans celebrate by eating the same thing: turkey. Sure, each family has its own traditions and dishes, but at some point in the day, we all sit down to the same main event. But this year might be different. In this chapter, I share my favorite recipes for simple sides that are **so delicious, they just might steal the show.**

harvest feast

Mashed Sweet Potatoes

You might not recognize sweet potatoes at your holiday table because they are in disguise: dressed up with sugar and marshmallows and more. But have you ever tried this subtly sweet tuber on its own? This Thanksgiving, give the potato a chance to shine with its beautiful simplicity. When you serve this dish, tell your guests that it is accentuated with just a hint of orange flavor and the aromatic pulse of nutmeg to give it a wafting allure. They may not know what it means, but they'll be as impressed with your chef-speak as they are with your dish!

Prep: 20 minutes / Cook: 40 minutes / Serves: 6–8

2 pounds sweet potatoes

salt

juice of 1 orange

¼ cup plain Greek yogurt

grated nutmeg

TRY THIS! TOPPING THIS DISH WITH SOME PECAN PIECES ADDS A WONDERFUL TEXTURE AND BALANCE TO THE SWEETNESS OF THE POTATO.

① Peel the potatoes, then cut them into large chunks.

② Place the potatoes in a large pot and cover them with water. Season generously with salt and add the orange juice. Cook over high heat until the water comes to a boil.

③ Turn the heat down to low and let simmer until the potatoes are soft but not yet falling apart, about 20–30 minutes. Drain and let cool for a few minutes.

④ Place the potatoes back into the pot and add the yogurt. Using a large spoon or a fork, mash the potatoes and stir to combine the yogurt so that you have a smooth puree.

⑤ Place into a serving dish and garnish with the nutmeg. Serve hot.

Cranberry-Pear Sauce

When you think of cranberry sauce, does it bring to mind the image of purple jelly from a can? The truth is that cranberry sauce doesn't have to be a sad afterthought, nor is it a time-consuming undertaking that will make you wish you had just bought a can. In fact, in this recipe the tart-sweetness of the cranberries combined with the delicious crunch of the pear will be the hit of the table—so give it a shot this Thanksgiving!

Prep: 10 minutes / Cook: 50 minutes / Chill: Overnight / Serves: 4

1 pound fresh cranberries

12 ounces orange juice

2 underripe pears, peeled and diced

½ cup walnut pieces

¼ cup maple syrup

1. Combine the cranberries and the orange juice in a medium-size pot. Cook over medium heat for about 25–40 minutes, or until the berries begin to burst and the sauce begins to thicken (the amount of time varies depending on the ripeness of the cranberries).

2. Reduce the heat to low and add the pears, walnuts, and maple syrup. Stir to combine and cook for another 10 minutes.

3. Remove from the heat and allow it to cool to room temperature. Then place the sauce in a covered dish in the refrigerator overnight. Allow the dish to warm back up to room temperature before serving.

AN ESTIMATED 21 MILLION POUNDS OF CRANBERRY SAUCE IS EATEN EACH THANKSGIVING.

IT TAKES ABOUT 36 APPLES TO MAKE ONE GALLON OF APPLE CIDER.

Hot Cinnamon Apple Cider

The cool of autumn nights calls for a steaming mug of cider to help warm the body. This drink is fun to put together, and it makes your whole house smell like an apple orchard. Bonus: It's so easy, your little brother or sister could do it.

Prep: 5 minutes / Cook: 20 minutes / Serves: 4

1 lemon

1 orange

1 quart apple cider

5 allspice berries

3 cloves

1 cinnamon stick

1. Juice the lemon and orange into a medium-size pot, placing the skin of half the lemon and half the orange in the pot with the juice. Discard the other half. Add the cider, allspice, and cinnamon and place the pot on the stove over medium heat.

2. Once the cider begins to steam and you begin to smell the yummy scents, turn the heat to low and simmer for another 10–15 minutes for the flavors to fully combine.

3. With a ladle, spoon the cider into mugs and enjoy while cuddled next to a fire or on a walk in the chill evening.

harvest feast

Tilly's Gingersnaps

This is my wife's great-grandmother's recipe, and every time that we make this, it brings back happy memories of time spent with family. To me, it is a great way to finish up a Thanksgiving feast. These sweet and spicy cookies smell so good that you won't want to wait for dessert!

Prep: 30 minutes /
Cook: 20 minutes /
Makes: 30–40 cookies

¾ cup butter

2 cups sugar

2 eggs

½ cup molasses

2 tablespoons apple cider vinegar

2 tablespoons powdered ginger

½ teaspoon salt

2 teaspoons baking soda

4 cups flour

¼ cup coarse sugar

1. Preheat your oven to 350 degrees. In a mixer (or bowl if using a hand mixer), beat together on medium speed the butter and the sugar. When they are thoroughly mixed, add the eggs one at a time, mixing until they are fully blended. With the mixer running, add the molasses, vinegar, and powdered ginger. In a separate bowl, mix the salt, baking soda, and flour. With the mixer running on low speed, slowly add the dry ingredients and mix until they're fully incorporated.

2. Remove the dough from the mixer and let sit for 10 minutes. Form the dough into small balls about the size of a walnut. Place on a baking tray lined with parchment paper and gently press the dough balls down to flatten them just a little. Sprinkle the coarse sugar on the top of each cookie.

3. Bake for 12 minutes. Remove from the oven and, using a spatula, move the cookies to a cooling rack.

BONUS TIP: If you have leftover dough, roll it into a tube shape, wrap it with plastic wrap, and freeze until you are ready to bake again.

GINGER
Eating ginger can ease a stomachache.

CHEW ON THIS

MOLASSES
On June 15, 1919, a massive storage container full of molasses burst in Boston, Massachusetts, sending an eight-foot wave of the sticky stuff coursing through the streets at 35 miles an hour. This event became known as the "Boston Molasses Disaster."

BUTTER
Ancient Romans did not eat butter. Instead, they used it to dress wounds.

Volunteering

During the holidays we celebrate our good fortune to be surrounded by loving family, to have a meal on the table, and to have friends to share it with. But we also use this time to remember that not all people have the same blessings. Take some time this season to give back to your community. Serving those in need, whether it is sharing a meal or simply sitting down to have a conversation with those who aren't able to be with their loved ones, is an opportunity to learn from and connect to the people who surround us in our everyday lives but with whom we rarely have contact. The blessings we are so fortunate to have are all the sweeter when we share them with others.

green scene

Create a **Green** Thanksgiving

Thanksgiving and other harvest feasts are a time to give thanks, so why not show the Earth some gratitude this year? Prepare an eco-friendly celebration that even Mother Nature would be proud of. Here are some small things you can do to make a difference.

1

BRING YOUR OWN BAG
Shop for the holidays with a reusable fabric bag. You'll help reduce the millions of plastic bags that make their way to landfills, waterways, and oceans each year.

2

TURN DOWN THE HEAT
With all the heat produced from cooking a giant feast, your house will be warmer than usual. Turn down the thermostat at least 2 degrees.

3

LET'S TALK TURKEY
The big meal is over, so what do you do with all the leftover turkey? Don't let it go to waste. Turn the page for some great ideas.

4

MAKE GREEN DECORATIONS
Make your own festive holiday decorations. Create a colorful center-piece using fruits and vegetables that you can eat later.

DITCH THE PAPER NAPKINS

5

Chowing down on all that delicious food can get messy, so use cloth napkins rather than paper, which can be washed and reused.

CUISINE SCENE

Mitsitam Restaurant

Long before the European settlers reached the shores here in America, there were thriving nations of Native Americans who lived off the bounty of the land and sea. At the Mitsitam Native Foods Cafe in the Native American Museum in Washington, D.C., these foods and indigenous food cultures are celebrated as part of this nation's heritage. The foods served include ingredients found from the Northern Woodlands areas of Minnesota and the Chesapeake Bay to the Great Plains and the Pacific Northwest. Food has always been a major part of the history of this land, and to eat these foods is to step back in time to an America before Columbus set foot here. The name Mitsitam means "let's eat" in the native tongue of two Northeastern tribes. Exploring history through food? Sounds like a great idea to me. Let's eat!

challenge

Leftovers Bonanza

On Thanksgiving you might feast to your heart's content, but on the day after it's tough to even look at cranberry sauce or stuffing. Three days later? Forget about it. So what do you do with all those leftovers?

This month, challenge yourself to see how creative you can be with your leftovers. The day after Thanksgiving (or any time when you have lots of extra food!), plan on making meals with your leftovers for the next five days. You can use extra turkey to make turkey noodle soup or delicious turkey chili. Try creating your own Thanksgiving sandwich, or see if you can whip up a salad using those leftover Brussels sprouts! At the end of five days, rate yourself to see how many times you actually used your leftovers. How did you do? Find out how you score on the Chef-O-Meter.

CHEF-O-METER

0–1 Meals
Disinterested Diner

You prefer not to eat the same thing too many times in a row. Try freezing your leftovers so that you can eat them again at your leisure. Or cook a big batch of something—turkey soup, for example—and then freeze that!

2–3 Meals
Growing Gourmand

You enjoy your leftovers, but you still like variety. Try finding meals that trick your taste buds into thinking you're eating something completely new. For example, turkey tacos are just the thing to spice it up!

4–5 Meals
Creative Cook

You manage to think of creative ways to use leftovers so that each meal becomes something completely different. You love experimenting and creating new meals, and it shows!

Holiday Celebration

Earth-Friendly Holidays

Start a Cooking Club!

December

—when the holidays are here—is the season to celebrate. Parties are thrown, families come together from places far and wide. Food is always at the center of these family gatherings because a shared meal is the best way to make people feel at home. Meals around the holidays tend to be feasts full of rich and delicious foods that warm the body as much as the spirit. Imagine how impressed your **grandparents will be when you do the cooking yourself!**

holiday
celebration

New England
Pot Roast

In New England, pot roast is a traditional holiday meal. It's also wonderfully easy to make! It was invented for just that purpose—throw everything together in one pot and let it cook until all the flavors come together. It takes a few hours to cook, but hey, they're not hours that you have to spend standing over the stove. Instead, use that time to make holiday cards!

Prep: 20 minutes / Cook: About 4 hours / Serves: 4 (with leftovers!)

2 pounds beef chuck roast

salt

pepper

2 tablespoons cooking oil

6 stalks celery, cut into 1-inch sections

6 carrots, peeled and cut into 1-inch sections (or a few handfuls of baby carrots)

1 pound potatoes, cut into 1-inch chunks

1 can (28 ounces) diced, peeled tomatoes

1 Preheat your oven to 275 degrees. Season the beef with the salt and pepper.

2 Heat a large ovenproof pot (one made entirely of metal with no plastic parts that could melt) over high heat. Add the oil, and when it is smoking hot, carefully add the beef. Cook it over high heat without moving it to give the meat a deep, caramelized crust. Turn the beef to another side and reduce the heat to medium.

3 Add the celery and carrot and stir to coat in the oil. Cook for another 5 minutes until the vegetables just begin to soften. Add the potatoes, tomatoes, and 1 cup of water and season again with salt.

4 Cover the pot and place it in the oven for 3½ hours. Then remove it from the oven and check the tenderness of the beef with a knife. You should be able to slice it easily. If it is not quite tender, replace the cover and cook for another 30–60 minutes.

5 Remove the pot from the oven and allow to cool for about 30 minutes. Remove the beef to a platter and slice it thinly. Place the vegetables around the beef and serve hot.

CUISINE SCENE

A Cultural Melting Pot

America is often referred to as a "melting pot"—a country made up of all different kinds of people and nationalities. Because of this, traditional holiday meals across America tend to vary by location, influenced by the people who originally settled there. The New England pot roast was actually inspired by a colonial adaptation of the European method of braising meats. On the other hand, Christmas dinner in Texas, which was once part of Mexico, often involves tamales! And celebrations in New Orleans usually include Creole gumbo—a hearty French-based stew flavored with African veggies and spices. The next time your family cooks a traditional holiday dish, try to figure out where the recipe came from.

Sweet Potato Latkes

Potato latkes (pancakes) are a tasty traditional Hanukkah treat. This take on the classic dish uses sweet potatoes, which have a little less water than regular potatoes, so I find them a little bit easier to work with. The cooking method for this requires frying the pancakes in hot oil, so this is definitely a dish to make with an adult.

Prep: 25 minutes / Cook: 20 minutes / Serves: 4

1 pound washed, unpeeled sweet potatoes

2 eggs, beaten

2 teaspoons onion powder

2 teaspoons salt

⅓ cup flour

¾ cup vegetable oil

1 Use a cheese or vegetable grater to grate your potatoes into shreds. Position the grater in a bowl and hold it steady with one hand and stroke the potato in a downward motion across the grate. Shreds will form under the grater and drop into the bowl. This process can take a while and wear out your arm. Take breaks or ask a sibling or parent to switch off with you. Also, be careful when you get to the end of the potato—you don't want to grate your fingers! When it gets too thin to grate, start a new potato.

2 When your potatoes are shredded, gently mix together all the ingredients except the oil in a large bowl. Be careful to eliminate all lumps of flour without mashing the potato up too much. Let the mixture sit for a few minutes for the flour to absorb the moisture from the potatoes and eggs. Put the mixture into a large gallon-size ziplock bag and seal the bag.

3 **PARENT'S HELP REQUIRED:** Preheat a large nonstick frying pan over medium-high heat. Add the oil and allow it to come to temperature. Using scissors, cut one corner of the bag to make a hole about 1 inch across. Squeeze the mixture into the pan to make little pancakes about 2 inches in size. Do not over-crowd the pan by putting in too many pancakes. Cook a few at a time, and when they are golden brown on one side, carefully flip them over and cook the other side until they're golden brown, about 3–4 minutes per side, depending on the heat of your pan. Remove the pancakes to a layer of paper towels. Once the oil is absorbed, remove the paper towels and put the pancakes in an oven set to low to keep them warm while you cook the remaining batches.

4 Serve the latkes plain or with sour cream and applesauce.

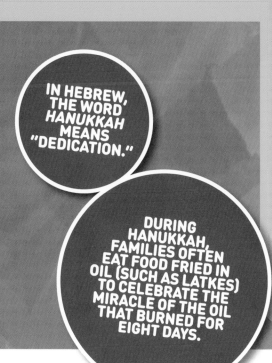

IN HEBREW, THE WORD HANUKKAH MEANS "DEDICATION."

DURING HANUKKAH, FAMILIES OFTEN EAT FOOD FRIED IN OIL (SUCH AS LATKES) TO CELEBRATE THE MIRACLE OF THE OIL THAT BURNED FOR EIGHT DAYS.

holiday
celebration

Crisp Oven Broccoli

Hate soft and mushy broccoli? That might be because, like most people, you like some crunch to your food. Here's my solution: Steam your vegetables to get them a little soft, and then throw them under the broiler until they are nice and crispy. It works for almost any vegetable and is an easy way to reintroduce yourself to ingredients that you thought you didn't like.

Prep: 10 minutes / Cook: 20 minutes / Serves: 4

salt

1 pound broccoli florets

2 tablespoons olive oil

1 Preheat your broiler to high. Bring a large pot of water to a boil. Generously season the water with salt.

2 When it is at a full boil, add the broccoli and cook until it is just beginning to soften and the florets are fragile, about 2–5 minutes, depending on the size of your florets. Drain and lay the broccoli out on a baking tray. Allow it to dry on the countertop for about 5 minutes.

3 Drizzle the broccoli with the olive oil and place the whole tray under the broiler, and just let it cook. Yes, it will start to get a little black, but that's not a bad thing; that's what gives it flavor!

4 When the broccoli is crispy and well colored, after about 10 minutes, remove it from the broiler and prepare to be amazed.

BONUS TIP! IF YOUR OVEN DOESN'T HAVE A BROILER, JUST SET THE TEMPERATURE AS HIGH AS IT WILL GO.

Poached Pears With Ice Cream

This is one of the most elegant desserts, and it is so easy to prepare—it's also sure to wow your friends. I like to serve it with a swoosh of Greek yogurt or sour cream, but a little ice cream never hurt anyone. So go ahead and pick your favorite.

Prep: 10 minutes / Cook: 1 hour / Serves: 4

4 pears, slightly underripe

1 quart pomegranate juice (you can also use cherry or grape juice, though you will need to dilute them with water by half)

1 lemon, cut in half

1 tablespoon vanilla extract

1 cinnamon stick

3 cloves

① Peel the pears and then cut them in half from top to bottom. Use a spoon to remove just the seed ball. Place the pears in a medium-size pot just big enough to hold them. Add the lemon halves, juice, vanilla, cinnamon, and cloves and place the pot over medium heat. When the liquid just begins to steam, cover the pot and reduce the heat to low. Cook for about 45 minutes and then test the pears to see if they are cooked. They should be tender but not falling apart.

② When the pears are cooked, remove them from the liquid with a slotted spoon and set them aside. Reduce the liquid by cooking it over medium heat until it begins to thicken just a little, about 15 minutes. Return the pears to the liquid and allow to cool.

③ Serve each person two pear halves drizzled with a little of the poaching liquid. Finish it off with the yogurt, sour cream, or ice cream topping of your choice.

THE WORD KWANZAA COMES FROM A SWAHILI PHRASE MEANING "FRUITS OF THE HARVEST."

DURING KWANZAA, PEOPLE DISPLAY MAZAO, FRUITS OF THE EARTH, TO REPRESENT UNITY AND PURPOSE.

green
scene

Earth-Friendly Holidays

The holiday season is all about family and celebration, but—let's face it—the gifts aren't too bad either. This season, why not give a gift to the planet by going green? You'll really be giving a present to yourself too ... A happy, healthy Earth! Try these easy steps to cut down on waste.

RECYCLED FRUITCAKE? AND YOU THOUGHT IT WAS BAD THE FIRST TIME AROUND! IN 2005, COLORADO RESIDENT BARBARA BAILEY STARTED THE GREAT FRUIT-CAKE RECYCLING PROJECT TO PREVENT UNWANTED CHRISTMAS CAKES FROM ENDING UP IN LANDFILLS. SIMPLY SHIP YOUR CAKE TO HER AND SHE WILL FIND IT A GOOD HOME.

WHAT TO DO

1 USE LED LIGHTS.
Decorate your tree and house this holiday season with energy-saving LED lights instead of incandescent ones. They're about 90 percent more efficient and can last much longer.

2 GIVE A GREEN GIFT.
Each week between Thanksgiving and New Year's, Americans produce an extra million tons of trash. You can make a difference by wrapping presents with recycled gift wrap. Send homemade cards made from materials you already have. Make gift coupons that promise you will make beds, wash dishes, and empty trash. Try to make recycled presents.

3 SQUASH YOUR TRASH.
Larger items in your trash cans take up a lot of room. Reduce the volume of things such as milk jugs and cereal boxes by stepping on them. Compacting trash cuts down the number and size of garbage bags your family uses.

4 LET IT COOL.
Let hot food and drinks cool to room temperature before placing them in the refrigerator. Hot items cause the internal fridge temperature to rise. It takes extra energy for the appliance to return to its original temperature setting.

5 PICK UP A PEN.
Whether you're campaigning for better recycling programs or a park cleanup day, make your voice heard. If you think your local government officials should take more action to help protect the environment, write them a letter making positive suggestions.

December challenge

Start a Cooking Club!

Food is delicious, sure, but one of the great joys of cooking is sharing it with others. Besides, it's only fair that you get to show off what you've learned! This month, your challenge is to start a cooking club and invite your friends to join. Kind of like a book club—but with food!

1 Decide how many times you want to meet, whether it is once a month or more often. Each month, have someone pick either a recipe for everyone to try to master or a general theme (such as fruit or holiday recipes).

2 At the next meeting, everyone brings in their own version of the dish. Sample all the dishes, and award prizes to each, such as "most creative," "weirdest," "healthiest," and "most delicious." Or if you have the space, you can all get together to cook the recipe!

3 Then rate how you did. Are you a beginner, intermediate, or master chef? Share what you thought was difficult or easy, and make sure to let your friends in on any cooking tips you discovered! Make sure to rotate who chooses the theme each meeting.

FRIENDS, FOOD, AND FUN ... WHAT COULD BE BETTER?

People Profile

Haile Thomas

Meet a 13-year-old chef from Tucson, Arizona. Haile began cooking at just 5 years old by watching cooking shows with her mom and getting involved in the kitchen. "My mom trusted me to help with the seasoning, mixing, chopping, and of course, tasting." When Haile was 9, she was able to cook full meals on her own. She credits early exposure to cooking as fueling her interest. She's accomplished a lot in just 13 years. She has founded advocacy groups such as the HAPPY Organization, the HEAL Festival, and the Healthy Belly Community Dinner, all of which promote healthy (and delicious!) eating habits. Haile uses these platforms to engage, educate, and inspire kids to make healthy lifestyle choices. She hopes (after earning a degree in nutrition) to turn her motivational-speaking expertise into a food-focused talk show.

Haile has many tips for aspiring kid chefs: "To start, make an effort to eat outside the typical 'kids menu box.' Expose yourself to new and different flavors and cuisines, and don't be afraid to mix it up in the kitchen. The more you experiment and get creative with a variety of fruits, veggies, spices, and herbs, the more recipes, flavor combinations, and new favorites you can discover!"

resources

If you're interested in learning more about Barton Seaver, cooking, or having a healthy and active lifestyle, grab a parent and check out the following websites for some great ideas!

Barton Seaver
www.bartonseaver.org

The HAPPY Organization
Inspiring Healthy Active Positive
Purposeful Youth!
www.thehappyorg.org

The HEAL Festival
Healthy Eating Active Lifestyle
www.healfestival.com

Resources for educators, families, and students who want to learn more about food are available at:

www.natgeoed.org/food

www.natgeofood.com

www.natgeoseafood.com

For online recipes and more "Chew on This" from *National Geographic Kids* magazine, check out:

www.kids.nationalgeographic.com

For fun family food ideas and recipes, go to:

ChopChopKids
www.chopchopmag.org

The Great Fruitcake Recycling Project
www.fruitcakerecycling.com

Additional Books by Barton Seaver:

Foods for Health: Choose and Use the Very Best Foods for Your Family and Our Planet
National Geographic Books, 2014

Where There's Smoke: Simple, Delicious, Sustainable Grilling
Sterling Epicure, 2013

For Cod and Country: Simple, Delicious, Sustainable Cooking
Sterling Epicure, 2011

Answers to the lunchbox quiz on page 117

1. **B** This mealtime master is definitely on the right track! Bonus points for the whole grain bread, fruit, and healthy popcorn as a salty snack. The cookies for dessert are a bit of a splurge, but it's okay to eat sweets on occasion as long as you balance them out with healthier items.

2. **A** The owner of this lunch is a cafeteria rock star! The veggie-packed wrap on a healthy tortilla is an awesome idea for mixing up a mundane meal. The carrots, grapes, and applesauce are terrific good-for-you choices. And the nuts will keep this eater powered up until dinner!

3. **D** Talk about a bogus box—but you probably already knew that, right? It's true, everything is okay in moderation, but if you're eating a lunch filled with sugar, salt, and not much else, you are going to feel run down, sluggish, and slow all afternoon. This lunch might be a short-term solution to hunger, but aside from the sandwich, there's nothing in here to keep you going!

4. **C** You're probably thinking this one looks *exactly* like the B lunch. You may have even graded them the same. But we spot one tiny problem: chips *and* cookies. This lunch has plenty going for it, and if you swap one of the less healthy items out for a yogurt or trail mix, you're definitely headed in the right direction.

acknowledgments

For Sam, Nik, Jane, Walt, and Amos —B. S.

The author would like to thank Becky Baines, Jennifer Emmett, Eva Absher-Schantz, Michael Piazza, Julia Nicolaysen, the New England Aquarium, his colleagues at the Center for Health and the Global Environment, and his wife, Carrie Ann.

The publisher would like to thank Barton Seaver for his hard work, his creative vision, his passion for finding community through cooking, and for his delicious food; Carrie Ann Seaver for her patience and support; Julia Nicolaysen for making things run smoothly; food photographer Michael Piazza and his assistant Erica Cole for their stunning work; scene photographer Lori Epstein for her vision and expertise; and stylist Stara Pezeshkian and her assistant Ashleigh Angel for organizing chaos.

Thanks also go to recipe testers Angela Modany, Bianca Bowman, Margaret Leist, Julide Dengel, Kelley Miller, Callie Broaddus, Lindsay Anderson, Marfé Ferguson Delano, Hannah August, Sara Zeglin, Lori Epstein, Hillary Leo, Jay Sumner, Kate Olesin, Catherine Hughes, Ruth Chamblee, Erica Green, Jennifer Emmett, Eva Absher-Schantz, Kay Boatner, Emma Rigney, Ariane Szu-Tu, Rachel Buchholz and Joe Guinto, Mary Jo Slazak, Laura Goertzel, Priyanka Sherman, Grace Hill, Tammi Colleary, Stephanie Rudig, and Joanne Baines for making sure each dish was a family-friendly hit.

Thanks to Anne McCormack, Sara Zeglin, and Tracy Hamilton Stone for polling the recipe selection with our kid audience to make sure we hit the right notes. And to Anne and Bob Emmett, Ellie and Carroll Nordoff, and the Flanigan family for the use of their kitchens during the scene photo shoots.

A very special thanks to the terrific kid models for making the most fun out of a very long day: Kylie Baxley, Katherine Bodner, David Bodner, Sarah Bodner, Joaquin Klossner, Jamai Williams, and Jameer Williams.

index

Boldface indicates illustrations.

recipes

credits

All food photography by Michael Piazza unless otherwise noted below.

SS: Shutterstock / IS: iStockphoto
NGS: National Geographic Society

Front cover (letters, salt shaker), Becky Hale & Mark Thiessen/NGS; (tablecloth), Jjustas/SS; (water), Mariyana Misaleva/SS; (napkin), cosma/SS; (banana), urfin/SS; (fork), MarFot/SS; (plate), Vitaly Korovin/SS; Spine: (fork), MarFot/SS; Back cover (peach & salad), Michael Piazza; author photo courtesy Barton Seaver; Jacket flaps: (chopping, hummus, salad & cookie), Michael Piazza; (boys), Lori Epstein/NGS

All tablecloths on chapter openers by Jjustas/SS.

All plates on chapter openers by Vitaly Korovin/SS.

All food letters on chapter openers by Becky Hale & Mark Thiessen/NGS.

FRONT MATTER: 2 (water), Mariyana Misaleva/SS; 2 (salt), Becky Hale & Mark Thiessen/NGS; 2 (fork), MarFot/SS; 2 (napkin), cosma/SS; 3 (banana), urfin/SS; 4 (dog), Javier Brosch/SS; 6 (asparagus), Lightspring/SS; 7 (asparagus), Lightspring/SS; 7 (A), Firmafotografen/IS; 7 (B), verani/IS; 7 (C), Gary Alvis/IS; 7 (D), cotesebastien/IS; 7 (E), Saturated/IS; 7, Gruffi/SS; 7 (G), ewg3D/IS; 7 (H), Helen Shorey/IS; 7 (I), bonchan/IS; 7 (J), Coprid/IS; 7 (K), emyerson/IS; 7 (L), huePhotography/IS; 7 (M), unalozmen/IS; 7 (N), Snappy_girl/IS; 7 (O), milosluz/IS; 7 (P), schamie/IS; 7, Lim Chew How/SS; 8 (A), gregdh/IS; 8 (B), Roxana_ro/IS; 8 (C), Edward Westmacott/IS; 8 (D), igartist/IS; 8 (E), Pinnacle-Marketing/IS; 8 (F), andrew burgess/IS; 8 (G), TeplouhovJurij/IS; 8 (H), Brotzler/IS; 9, Lightspring/SS **JANUARY:** 10 (UP), Juergen Richter/LOOK/Getty Images; 10 (LO), Lori Epstein/NGS; 11, fotohunter/SS; 12, Juergen Richter/LOOK/Getty Images; 13, Elena Schweitzer/SS; 13, barbaliss/SS; 15, barbaliss/SS; 16, Lori Epstein/NGS; 17, barbaliss/SS; 17, barbaliss/SS; 20, Lori Epstein/NGS; 21, Lori Epstein/NGS **FEBRUARY:** 22 (CTR), Becky Hale & Mark Thiessen/NGS; 22 (LO), Lori Epstein/NGS; 23, art_of_sun/SS; 25 (UP), bonchan/SS; 25, art_of_sun/SS; 26, Lori Epstein/NGS; 27 (UP), Lu Mikhaylova/SS; 27 (LO), Dionisvera/SS; 31, Becky Hale & Mark Thiessen/NGS; 32, Lori Epstein/NGS **MARCH:** 34 (UP), Thomas Barwick/Stone Sub/Getty Images; 34 (CTR), Becky Hale & Mark Thiessen/NGS; 34, clickclick/IS; 35, Molodec/SS; 36, Thomas Barwick/Stone Sub/Getty Images; 37 (UP), Javier Brosch/SS; 38, v.s.anandhakrishna/SS; 39 (UP), Sergey Zavalnyuk/IS; 39 (RT), Hulton Archive/Getty Images; 40, Lightspring/SS; 41,

Lori Epstein/NGS; 42, Becky Hale & Mark Thiessen/NGS; 43 (UPLE), Ivan Hunter/Digital Vision/Getty Images; 43 (UPRT), senk/SS; 43 (LO), ColorBlind Images/Iconica/Getty Images; 44 (A), og-vision/IS; 44 (B), fotogal/IS; 44 (C), YinYang/IS; 44 (D), YinYang/IS; 44 (E), Oliver Hoffmann/IS; 44 (F), Kasiam/IS; 44 (G), YinYang/IS; 44 (H), Joe Biafore/IS; 44 (I), Riverlim/IS; 45 (J), lightshows/IS; 45 (K), rimglow/IS; 44 (L), cclickclick/IS; 45 (background), Riverlim/IS **APRIL:** 46 (LO), Lori Epstein/NGS; 47, Keith Publicover/SS; 49, Dimj/SS; 54-55, Arco Images GmbH/Alamy; 55, ifong/SS; 56 (UP), Kim Nguyen/SS; 56 (CTR), Dima Sobko/SS; 56 (LO), Valery/SS, 56, Lori Epstein/NGS; 57 (UP), Svitlana-ua/SS; 57 (CTR), Nattika/SS **MAY:** 58 (CTR & LO), Lori Epstein/NGS; 59, vlad09/SS; 61, Melica/SS; 61 (LO), Gertan/SS; 62 (UP), Diana Taliun/SS; 65 (CTR), Olga Miltsova/SS; 66, Lori Epstein/NGS; 66, Lori Epstein/NGS; 67, Tyler Golden/NBC/Getty Images; 68-69, Sebastien Burel/SS; 69, Lori Epstein/NGS **JUNE:** 70 (CTR), Brian J. Skerry/National Geographic Creative; 70 (LO), Volosina/SS; 71, Javier Brosch/SS; 73 (RT), S-F/SS; 73 (flames), hugolacasse/SS; 74 (flames), hugolacasse/SS; 74, Westend61/Getty Images; 75 (flames), hugolacasse/SS; 76 (flames), hugolacasse/SS; 78-79, Brian J. Skerry/National Geographic Creative; 78 (INSET), Cubolmages srl/Alamy; 80 (A), Maris Kiselov/SS; 80 (B), Alasdair Thomson/IS; 80 (C), Jiri Hera/SS; 80 (D), Andrii Gorulko/SS; 81 (A), Stephanie Frey/SS; 81 (B), julie deshaies/SS; 81 (C), stocksolutions/SS; 81 (D), HomeStudio/SS; 81 (E), phloen/SS; 81 (F), Volosina/SS; 81 (G), amenic181/SS; 81 (H), amenic181/SS; 81, Photo courtesy of Eyak Preservation Council **JULY:** 82, (UP) Brian Hagiwara Studio/age fotostock; 82 (CTR), Eric Audras/Onoky/Getty Images; 82 (LO), Lori Epstein/NGS; 83, koosen/SS; 84, Brian Hagiwara Studio/age fotostock; 85 (LO), Robyn Mackenzie/SS; 87 (UP), Angel Simon/SS; 87 (LO), Ufuk ZIVANA/SS; 88, aa3/SS; 90-91, Eric Audras/Onoky/Getty Images; 91 (UP), Africa Studio/SS; 92 (UP), Blend Images - KidStock/Brand X/Getty Images; 92 (LOLE), Carlos Caetano/SS; 92 (LO), Deborah Jaffe/Blend Images RM/Getty Images; 93, Lori Epstein/NGS; 93 (RT), spinetta/SS **AUGUST:** 94 (CTR), Andreas Wonisch/Flickr RF/Getty Images; 94 (LO), Lori Epstein/NGS; 95, AllaR15/SS; 97, cosma/SS; 98, Lori Epstein/NGS; 99 (UP), Madlen/SS; 101, Fancy Collection/SuperStock; 102-103, Andreas Wonisch/Flickr RF/Getty Images; 103, Becky Hale & Mark Thiessen/NGS; 104-105, Peshkova/SS; 105 (UP), Lim Chew How/SS; 105, Lori Epstein/NGS **SEPTEMBER:** 106 (CTR), Paul Marotta/Flickr Open/Getty Images; 106 (LO), Lori Epstein/NGS; 107, Elena Kharichkina/SS; 108, Bon Appetit/Alamy; 109 (tomato), Bozena Fulawka/SS; 110 (LE), Canadapanda/SS; 111 (tomato), Bozena Fulawka/SS; 111 (RT), Canadapanda/SS; 112 (UP), Paul Marotta/Flickr Open/Getty

Images; 113 (tomato), Bozena Fulawka/SS; 113, Gilles Mingasson/Figarophoto/Contour by Getty Images; 114, Becky Hale & Mark Thiessen/NGS; 115 (tomato), Bozena Fulawka/SS; 115, Rob Lewine/Tetra images RF/Getty Images; 116, Lori Epstein/NGS; 117, Lori Epstein/NGS; 117, Lori Epstein/NGS; 117 (UP), Alhovik/SS **OCTOBER:** 118 (LO), Lori Epstein/NGS; 119, Becky Hale & Mark Thiessen/NGS; 120, Lori Epstein/NGS; 121 (UP), Dan Kosmayer/SS; 126, Lori Epstein/NGS; 128, Lori Epstein/NGS; 129, Lori Epstein/NGS **NOVEMBER:** 130 (UP), Lori Epstein/NGS; 130 (CTR), Corbis/SuperStock; 130 (LO), Paula Hible/Photolibrary RM/Getty Images; 131, Lori Epstein/NGS; 132, Lori Epstein/NGS; 133, Lori Epstein/NGS; 134 (UP), EM Arts/SS; 138, Corbis/SuperStock; 138 (UP), Jetta Productions/Blend Images/Getty Images; 138 (CTR), Steve Lupton/Corbis; 138, Stockbyte/Brand X/Getty Images; 139, Image Source/SuperStock; 139 (RT), Chris Maddaloni/CQ-Roll Call/Getty Images; 140 (UP), Paula Hible/Photolibrary RM/Getty Images; 140 (CTR), Alexandra Grablewski/Lifesize/Getty Images; 140 (LO), imagebroker/Alamy; 141 (UP), Paula Hible/Photolibrary RM/Getty Images **DECEMBER:** 142 (CTR), Rudi Von Briel/Stockbyte/Getty Images; 142 (LO), Lori Epstein/NGS; 143, dny3d/ShutterPoint Photography; 145 (evergreens), S-F/SS, 145 (evergreens), S-F/SS, 145, Blend Images/Alamy; 146, James And James/Stockbyte/Getty Images; 146 (evergreens), S-F/SS; 147 (evergreens), S-F/SS; 147, James And James/Stockbyte/Getty Images; 148 (evergreens), S-F/SS; 149 (evergreens), S-F/SS; 150 (evergreens), S-F/SS; 150, Rudi Von Briel/Stockbyte/Getty Images; 151 (evergreens), S-F/SS; 152 (evergreens), S-F/SS; 152, Lori Epstein/NGS; 152, Lori Epstein/NGS; 153 (evergreens), S-F/SS; 153 (evergreens), S-F/SS; 153, courtesy of Charmaine Thomas **BACK MATTER:** 154, Michael Piazza; 154-155, MarFot/SS; 155 (UP), Vitaly Korovin/SS; 155 (LO), Cosma/SS; 160, Michael Piazza